"I Can See You Naked"

"I Can See You Naked"

A Fearless Guide to Making Great Presentations

by Ron Hoff

Andrews and McMeel

A Universal Press Syndicate Company

Kansas City ■ New York

Designed and illustrated by Barrie Maguire

Library of Congress Cataloging-in-Publication Data
Hoff, Ron.
  "I can see you naked"

  Bibliography: p.
  1. Public speaking I. Title.
PN4121.H457   1988   808.5'1   88-6300
ISBN 0-8362-7944-1
ISBN 0-8362-7946-8 (pbk.)
First Printing, March 1988
Second Printing, October 1990

Contents

PART SIX

How to deal with questions

PART SEVEN

Learning from those who cast a spell and stay with us forever.

PART EIGHT

Afterwards—*Some things to think about
that will make your next presentation even better.*

Prologue

"I Can See You Naked."

When you get up there on that platform, and you look out at your audience, let your imagination help you overcome your nervousness. Just scan your audience, moving back and forth, *until you see everybody naked.*"

"Why on earth would I want to do that?" the aspiring presenter asks.

"Because you can't be intimidated by naked people," the presentation coach explains. "Naked people are so vulnerable, so defenseless, that you will feel *superior* to them—"

"Because I'm fully clothed—"

"Exactly. You're clothed. They're naked. You're in control."

Lest you think that this is some sort of prank to get your attention in the opening moments of this book, let me assure you that this is no joke.

Visualizing audiences in the buff, as a counter to nervousness, has been taught by presentation experts for years. As a concept, it has reached almost classic scale—and I felt that any self-respecting book on presentation skills should discuss it.

I decided to go beyond discussion. I decided to research it—personally. I tried it three times—once on a bunch of bankers in New Hampshire; once on a convention of insurance agents (mostly women) in Chicago; and once on some advertising executives in the Bahamas. The results of all three experiments were roughly the same, but I had the most trouble with the insurance agents (I think they sensed what I was up to).

Here are the topline results of my research:

Talking to naked audiences can be distracting. You get up there, all primed to talk about marketing strategy or whatever, and you see this crowd of naked men and women staring back at you. They don't seem to realize that they're naked. Or if they do, it doesn't bother them. One lady of epic proportions jumped out of her chair to wave to a friend behind her, dropped her papers on the floor, prompting a kind old gentleman to get down on his hands and knees to help her. It was unforgettable. My subject flew right out the window, gone from my mind. But research is research—and you persevere. You look out at those cheery, amiable, helpful people—sitting there in their uncomprehending nakedness, and you don't feel nervous any more. You just feel *odd*. Different. Clothed. I couldn't handle it.

I decided, as a dutiful researcher, to try the same concept with underwear. I'd visualize the audience in their underwear, and of course I'd be standing there—dressed to the nines—in my best gray gabardines. This seemed better to me. Less eccentric. I wouldn't feel so guilty. I tried it.

I still couldn't remember what I was going to say. Have you ever tried to talk seriously to a woman in French lingerie, particularly if she's sitting next to a skinny guy in Fruit of the Loom(s)? It's unsettling. I concluded that undressed audiences, generally, aren't nearly as approachable as you might think. My advice is—*never talk to a naked audience.*

I've got some other research to share with you. Same subject—but different. Let me explain. I have now taught over two thousand business professionals how to make a presentation. Fully twenty-five of them have taken their clothes off while presenting. Though all of them were quite charming about it, and had interesting reasons for disrobing ("formal attire is hateful and uncomfortable," "don't judge people by what they wear to work")—there was a bewitching quality to the atmosphere. Something profound was happening.

I should add that these presentations are videotaped in front of live audiences. The tapes are available for historians to ponder.

Why all this interest in *nakedness* when people think of self-presentation? A psychologist would tell you that presentation offers a rare opportunity to act out fantasies—or to present ourselves, legitimately, in a way that is closer to our *real* selves than our workaday selves.

But it doesn't happen very often, does it? Most presenters seldom let their guards down.

Maybe they have realized something which audiences have been doing, rather covertly, for a long time.

Audiences can, with very little imagination, *visualize the presenter naked*. Audiences love to daydream anyway, and this merely adds a welcome bit of interest. The tables are turned!

And the *presenter* says, "I know what you're doing, you sly devils, and I can't let you do it. I can't risk the possibility of rejection."

"Oh, phooey," says the audience, "you're no fun."

And the presenter scrunches down behind the podium so no one can see him, reads from his script so he will say nothing spontaneous, keeps his eyes down so that no one can make contact, and holds his voice on one deadly level to muffle his emotions.

No fun.

This book is dedicated to the exhilaration of presenting well. And to making sure that *you* feel the joy of it.

—RON HOFF

PART ONE

"What *is* a presentation? What am I getting myself into?"

A NUGGET FOR YOUR NEXT PRESENTATION:
"Keep the ball _alive_."

Presentation is, more and more, a _visual_ medium. The audience thinks visually—and it will help you, the presenter, to think in terms of pictures. If a mental image helps you to hold a thought or concept in your brain, _use it!_ So it's a little weird or goofy. You're more likely to remember it. Besides, it's just for you. Here's a visual idea, a nugget that puts the whole subject of presentation into a picture. It's a bit weird, but it makes a point that could be useful in your next presentation.

NUGGET: Think of your next presentation as a big, buoyant medicine ball which you must keep "alive." It's your responsibility to keep that ball up in the air, guiding it deftly, tapping it ever higher, perhaps hitting it smartly with your head. Occasionally you'll boost the ball toward someone in your audience. That ball will move around a lot, people will get involved with it, but it will always come back to you—because you're the one who keeps it "alive." Besides, it's your ball.

1

What *is* a presentation? A surprising definition to improve your next one.

Y̲ou have been asked to make a *presentation*.

Consider yourself complimented.

Somebody thinks you know something that is worth hearing or seeing—probably both.

You have, in fact, entered a very charmed circle. The majority of people are never asked. They never hear those flattering, felicitous words, *"We'd like you to make a presentation to us."*

You accept. The date of the presentation seems quite remote— and you suspect it may never arrive at all.

The precise hour and place assume minor importance when the date is so far away—and you jot the particulars into your "plan ahead" calendar.

All goes well until several days prior to the presentation date.

Then comes the unsettling question, *"What have I let myself in for?"*

In struggling to deal with this issue, some people have even been known to admit, "I'm not sure I know what a presentation *is*. It sort of sounds like something that should be done in costume."

What *is* it anyway?

There are many things that a presentation is *not*, but it is *mainly* not "making a speech." The phrase even *sounds* archaic, and is probably best characterized by that sarcastic old taunt, "You're not going to *make a speech*, are you?" Speeches have a way of getting fat as they are being given, whereas presentations tend to skinny down to a sharp point. (The graphic on the following page will help you detect the difference. Madeliene Nagel, a New York marketing and media expert, suggested the "inside/out and outside/in" idea.)

You are part of the message of a presentation, just as surely as Marshall McLuhan said, "The medium is the message."

A few snapshots may be in order here—so that we don't fall too deeply into theoretical abstractions.

■ In Los Angeles, the treasurer of a midsized brokerage firm gets up before his executive committee to report that expenses are running far beyond budget and the committee should make immediate cutbacks. He is making a presentation.

■ Across the country, a group manager of a major oil company appears before the company's board of directors to recommend that a

new refinery be acquired in South America. She is making a presentation.

■ In Shaker Heights, Ohio, a woman rises to her feet to review the novel she has just read. Her book club settles back to listen. The woman is making a presentation.

■ On a nearby campus, a marketing student stands on a small platform in front of his Corporate Strategies class and dissects a case history. Summarizing, he tells what the bankrupt subject of the case *should have done*. He is making a presentation.

■ In Kansas City, an advertising agency art director submits a layout to a client and asks for approval to start production. She is making a presentation.

■ A few blocks away, a sales manager applies for an executive position with a rising computer software company. He is making a presentation.

■ Two presidential candidates, a New York Republican, and a Missouri Democrat, sit on the stage at Drake University and have a lively debate by satellite. One man presenting, and then the other, the exchange goes on for an hour. The evening is filled with presentations.

■ That same night, over a friendly bridge game with the neighbors, a husband in his sixties explains why he is voting Democratic, while his wife—at another table—tells why she couldn't possibly vote anything but Republican. Both of them are looking for converts. And both are making presentations.

■ If you really want to see presentations being made at their most demanding level, visit a courtroom. There, as an important trial unwinds, you will witness immaculately prepared presentations that are literally of life-or-death importance.

Sit there in the courtroom, or the conference room, or the "back room" of a political gathering and you will realize that two starkly simple and inherently dramatic developments are taking place during a winning presentation. One centers on the presenter. The other features the audience. And both things are happening simultaneously.

1. You, the presenter, are making a *commitment* to your audience that you can help them solve a problem—seize an opportunity—*do something they really want.*

2. The audience, meanwhile, is making a *judgment* on the value and validity of your promise.

"I will prove to your satisfaction that this man is innocent and should be allowed to return to his rightful place in society," says the defense attorney. The jury reacts to this commitment with a variety of thoughtful expressions, all saying, in one way or another, "Well, we'll see about that." And the commitment/judgment process begins.

"I will save your soul," vows the preacher, and his flock rouses itself, hoping against hope that this commitment can be achieved in the next thirty minutes, but reserving the right to dismiss it as an innocent case of evangelical puffery.

Commitment by the presenter.

Judgment by the audience.

"I will," says the presenter, moving forward.

"Let's see if you can," says the audience, leaning back, arms folded.

This simple identification of roles forces the presenter to set forth on a demanding mission. There is a clearly stated objective. It's not idle wool-gathering. It's not information-sharing. It's a serious, sincere *bid for conversion.*

By the end of the presentation, if the presenter has fulfilled his or her mission, the audience will uncross its arms and say, "By golly, I see what you mean. I agree."

Maybe our definition of a presentation can be boiled down to this handful of words:

A presentation is a commitment by the presenter to help the audience do something—and a constant, simultaneous evaluation of the worth of that commitment by the audience.

The beauty of this definition is that it's fairly short—and it keeps the presenter talking about the audience's self-interest rather than his (or her) own. Most presentations drone endlessly about the *presenter's* interests (with a generous portion of ego).

There's something else. The presenter can tell how the presentation is going, every step of the way, by merely looking at the audience.

The audience *shows you* how you're doing. It's all in the body language, and you'll know how to read it—as well as *facial* language—before you're halfway through this book.

But, first, see yourself as a presenter bringing things to a point—narrowing the options, helping your audience to arrive at a conclusion you believe in. You're talking to these nice people, one by one, and you can tell—with absolute accuracy—whether they're with you or not. Your mission is to win them all.

2

"I need you.
You need me."

No, that is not the whispered sentiment of a star-crossed lover. Nor is it part of a hurried conversation on the baseball field between pitcher and catcher.

It is the core of a relationship that should exist between presenter and audience.

It is important to any understanding of the dynamics of presentation because it suggests a partnership rather than a performance, a linkage rather than a confrontation, coming closer rather than pulling apart.

What we're talking about here is the heart of our headline: *needs*. No presentation should occur without them. Since they are so fundamental to the success of your next presentation, they deserve some thoughtful examination (and some graphics to stick in your mind):

Every presentation begins in this way. The audience *needs* something—usually *help*. (Ask a seasoned salesman what he wants to get out of a presentation and invariably he will say, "just give me *one* idea, that's all I ask, something I can use tomorrow.")

By coming to your presentation, by simply showing up, your audience is expressing a need for help, counsel, wisdom, inspiration—maybe even something that can change its life. Not its collective life—its personal, individual lives.

If truth be told, the audience arrives on the scene with the ardent hope that the presenter knows something that it does not.

Maybe the presenter has a secret, and is willing to share it with the audience. If not, the presenter may have a fresh way of looking at things—one that the audience can apply—profitably. Perhaps tomorrow.

The presenter has needs, too, of course. *Many.* But nothing quite equals the presenter's need for *approval.* Only the audience can give it, but it can be rendered in many forms—from a simple vote (a raising of hands), to a signature on a document (such as a long-term contract), to an outburst of applause.

Without some indication of approval, response, endorsement, confirmation—*something!*—the presenter is lost at sea, adrift, seeking a signal.

This can be tough on the ego. (*No* response is, in many ways, worse than outright rejection.) But it can also leave the presenter without authorization to *do anything.*

How many meetings have you left with the uneasy feeling that nobody had an inkling of what to do next?

This may not be the fault of the audience alone. Maybe the first link in our circuit was never made. Maybe the audience was there, registering a need, but the presenter did what thousands of presenters do: *talked about himself, or herself.* The audience withdrew, sensing that its need was being ignored. Here's what happens:

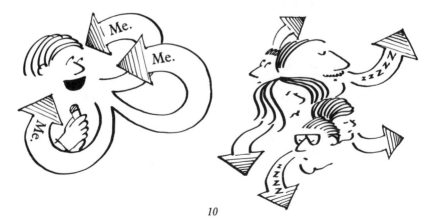

Nothing happens. The area between audience and presenter remains a void. *No needs are met.* No help is offered. No approval is given. Everybody goes home. Another useless meeting. The audience says, "Boy, was that a dreary meeting." The presenter says, "That audience was dead." The *fulfillment* of needs is essential.

■

Let's assume we've got our circuit going. The circulation in our circle of needs is flowing smoothly. There are no gaps, no hitches.

Gradually, a gratifying sense of *rapport* begins to fill the room. The distance between audience and presenter seems less.

The prognosis for this presentation looks very good indeed.

There are few things in life that can match the exhilaration of a meeting where everything is going well.

But, before the euphoria carries us blissfully away, is there nothing else? No other overriding need?

There is. However, it applies to *brilliant* presentations only. So, if you are simply striving for brilliance rather than insisting on it—consider the following "need" as an intriguing possibility and nothing more. If brilliance is *necessary* to you, listen up.

■

In every *brilliant* presentation, there is what Spalding Gray—the noted writer, actor, and monologist—calls "the perfect moment." He refers to it in his presentation of "Swimming to Cambodia"—a monologue which enjoyed great success at Lincoln Center in New York and, later, as a film. It's worth thinking about.

"The perfect moment" is a burst of incandescence that ignites the entire presentation and gives it an everlasting impression on the audience's memory.

"Swimming to Cambodia" demonstrated its own "perfect moment"—as performed by Mr. Gray—when he described his experience of swimming in the towering surf of the Indian Ocean.

Joe Froschl, an advertising agency executive in New York City, has his own language for this moment of enlightenment. He calls it "a flash of insight that gives us a reason to believe."

Fred Lemont, an experienced marketing consultant and exceptional presenter, calls it a dramatic point in a presentation "which everybody can rally 'round."

"A perfect moment" can be crafted into your presentation and rehearsed to perfection—or it may occur suddenly and spectacularly as an idea erupts in a shower of sparks.

"A perfect moment":

A young business executive named Richard Foody stands before us. He wears a dark blue suit and white shirt. He is nervous. He fluffs some words. He is going to tell us about skiing, but he is starting his presentation in the same way that he might approach a steep, downhill slope. *Very, very* carefully. He is telling us, rather matter-of-factly, that you need certain things before you can start to ski. Gloves. He slips them on. A ski cap. He pulls one over his ears. A number (skiing is like everything else, you have to have a number!).

He hangs the cardboard number around his neck (his coat has been discarded; his tie, loosened). Suddenly, he looks very different. A strangeness has set in—call it "a perfect moment," or at least the start of one. He crouches down, his eyes glistening, and describes the breathless anticipation of "pushing off." His body sways as he speeds down the slope. He's really into it—into his "moment"—carrying us with him. Then, astonishingly, *he falls down.* His feet fly out from under him, and he's down—in a heap. Right in front of us! He looks around, struggles to his feet, chuckles self-consciously. He starts talking to us again, like a stream of consciousness, words coming faster and much easier than before. He realizes he has almost completed his fearsome run down the slope—*and he's home, free!* Well, almost free. What's a little spill when you're out to conquer a mountain—and, most important, your own fears of it? He looks totally different now—confident, elated, in control. He rips off his number and holds it high over his head. There is a kind of radiant jubilation about him. "Just grab your number," he shouts, *"and go."*

Later, it dawned on me that he wasn't just talking about skiing, he was talking about "taking a chance"—doing something different—making a commitment to life. And, shortly thereafter, he moved on to a much bigger job with a different company.

"Perfect moments" may sound a bit weird, but they are very easy to identify. They tend to engulf audiences in a sudden awareness that something unusual has happened. They communicate on a higher level of involvement. And they often conclude in a feeling of emotional closeness between presenter and audience—as if they had shared some kind of transcendent experience.

The vital reminder

It's pleasant to think about the "perfect moments" of your life. It's fun to think about capturing one for your next presentation. But it's *vital* to remember what presentation is all about: *It's about meeting needs.* It's about completing the circle that revolves around rapport. It's the honest realization and resulting reward of "I need you. You need me."

3

Escaping the script.
An introduction to
nonverbal communication.

In the beginning, there was the script.

It was the exact text of the presentation, double- or triple-spaced by a manual typewriter on 8½″ × 11″ sheets of white paper.

It was generally stapled together by the typist so the speaker wouldn't lose the pages, or get them in the wrong order, on the way to the meeting.

Then, at the meeting, the speaker would pull the staples out of the script while standing behind the lectern. Unstapled, the pages could be moved off to the side after they were read.

(There were times when the speaker couldn't get the staples out—and he or she would flip the pages over the top of the lectern so that they dangled loosely on the other side. Audiences would frequently *count* the pages as they came over the top, guessing how many remained to be read. This often proved to be more interesting than listening to the speaker.)

Notes on 3″ × 5″ cards were a big step forward. They freed the speaker from the lectern. The cards could also be shuffled in moments of anxiety—but "notes" instead of a "script" conveyed a far more self-assured impression to the audience. (Scripts almost immediately beg the question, "I wonder if the speaker really wrote it.") Scripts and notes have also been known to raise questions about vitality and alertness.

The New York Times, commenting on President Reagan's visit to the Venice Summit Conference in mid-June of 1987, made this telling observation:

> "In private meetings at the Venice Summit Conference, President Reagan spoke from note cards prepared for him. He was the only one of the Western leaders unable or unwilling to exchange ideas—to talk about the issues—without a script. When the others tried to start a discussion about Mikhail Gorbachev, the president read them lines from one of his recent speeches."

This was the lead paragraph in a column by Anthony Lewis, regular *Times'* staffer.

In addition to words on paper, speakers have also been known to put memory-joggers on their cuffs, their fingernails, and their palms. (Anthony Quinn, the actor, revealed that he often writes one-word reminders on the tips of his fingers in order to emphasize certain qualities in his on-stage performances.) These jottings work with varying degrees of success—usually depending on the speaker's belief in their usefulness. Sweaty palms could also be a factor.

Television came along and introduced us to teleprompters, giant cue cards, and the like. Some of the nation's most heralded speakers have been known to position a script in front of them and turn a page every now and then while actually reading, word for word, from an off-camera teleprompter. This touch of craftiness led the audience to believe that the speaker knew his on-camera script *so well* that only a rare downward glance or page turn was necessary.

Television also brought us the *storyboard*—a sort of audio/visual device that enabled advertisers to get the gist of a commercial before it was produced.

The finished commercial frequently had all kinds of directorial touches to polish up the production values, but advertisers got an *impression* of the selling idea by studying the dozen or so frames on the "board."

A "key frame" was sometimes used to focus the message of the commercial even more vividly—and to make it easier for the advertiser to remember.

Enter Ben Goodspeed, a business analyst and author, who was a partner at a consulting company called Inferential Focus in New York City. Ben handed me the first *mindmap* I had ever seen. It was a relative of the storyboard, but it was uniquely different. *It was a visualization of a presentation*—and it was for the sole use of the presenter.

Ben's squiggly drawing had a kind of childlike charm to it. It had bursts of color, lines going every which way, and primitive pictures. I wasn't sure I totally understood its message (more about that in a minute), but it looked like a great leap forward for presenters.

It was a one-page picture of a presentation, a graphic roadmap, and—because it had been created by the presenter—it stuck in his mind like glue.

An easy way to think of this concept, and put it to work for you, is to ask yourself, "If my presentation were going to be laid out like a Monopoly board, or a Candy Land® board, or almost *any* kind of game board, what would it look like?"

This will get you thinking in terms of graphic relationships

© 1984 Milton Bradley Company, made in U.S.A. Candy Land is a registered trademark of Milton Bradley Company.

instead of word relationships, and it forces you to work on a single surface where you can see the whole thing at one time.

It is, essentially, a map—with graphics to help you see where you're going. The route is clearly indicated by little blocks of color leading you through such picturesque neighborhoods as the Peppermint Forest, the Lollipop Woods, the Ice Cream Sea, the Molasses Swamp, and so on.

The Candy Land game board, if studied as a way to remember your next presentation, can be a lively revelation.

Please note that each locality has a vivid *picture* and *illustrated* personality to remember it by.

Gloppy, a lovable brown lump, lives in the Molasses Swamp. Lord Licorice, dressed appropriately in black, lives in the Licorice Castle.

You get the idea. There's at least one picture per neighborhood. The course to be followed is colorfully clear. And the words are few but vibrant.

The whole board is a delightful piece of almost-instant communications, presented in the way that most people remember things, *nonverbally.*

Now, let me show you a raw example of a mindmap. It was sketched by the presenter for a presentation to the Young President's Organization in New York City. If you don't quite understand it, don't worry about it (nobody can really get inside somebody else's brain). Just consider the concept and what you might do with it.

Part Map, Part Picture, Part Game
—it's an easy way to visualize your next presentation.

This "Presentation on Perceptions" starts in the lower left (with the big eyeball)—swings up through the billboard (with the point of view)—moves quickly through the supporting exhibits (beginning with Gerald Ford's perception as being clumsy)—returns to the point of view—presents the idea (The Perception Process)—and closes in the lower right with "The Next Step . . ."

This is how the flow goes.

Don't try to understand this one—Try your own!

There aren't any rigid rules to follow in trying this exercise, but here are some "observations" you might want to consider.

1. Think of your presentation as a game board. Where would it start? What would you *see* along the way? What are the "neighborhoods" of importance?
2. Visualize the main components of your speech with your own graphics. The roughest sketches, the skinniest stick figures will be fine—just as long as they represent pictures in your mind.
3. Have a pathway, a route. Want to use green arrows? Traffic symbols? Big, blocky numbers? Or maybe the route is so obvious to you that you don't need any of those things. Whatever works for you, *do it*.
4. Keep everything on one surface. That doesn't mean you're prevented from attaching something to that surface—maybe a snapshot, a clipping, whatever. But the map should remain a single, self-contained piece of communication.
5. Don't worry with it. Have some fun with it. Think of Candy Land. Let it flow.

Once you've seen your presentation *as a picture*, you'll find that it's easy to bring it forward in your brain. It just *appears*, in all its glory, exactly the way you created it. It's always easier to remember what we create ourselves.

And if you feel that you need a little security blanket, a little memory reinforcement—*use the hand-drawn map of your presentation as a teleprompter.* Just put it off to one side, maybe on the floor, where you can glance at it if you need to. One glance and you'll know exactly where you are. More important, you'll see what comes *next*. And if anybody else sees it, there's nothing to worry about. You're the only one who knows what it is.

■

Now, one more option—another leap beyond the antiquated script.

Since everything has to have a name these days, let's call it a memory model. Reason: it provides a three-dimensional model for your memory to work with.

The memory model honors the technique of mindmapping and builds on it, takes it "public." Before that begins to sound like so much mumbo jumbo, let me give you a snapshot:

■ *A young executive walks into a client meeting with a mailbox under his arm.* It's one of those old, country mailboxes that holds a ton of mail. The presenter peers into the box and starts pulling stuff out. His presentation: How to communicate more effectively with direct mail.

What is this? *It's a "script" for the presenter, but the audience sees it differently.*

■ *Every piece that comes out of the mailbox triggers a point in the presenter's mind.* There's something very authentic about his presentation—it's all documented, demonstrated by real material. The audience doesn't realize it, but the presenter is being led through his presentation by the contents of the mailbox.

■ *The mailbox, and what's inside it, is a memory model, a map with a third dimension.* It is a "script" for the presenter that the audience sees as a realistic and maybe even a charming "prop."

The memory model. Before that begins to sound too pretentious, let's hurry on to some other examples.

■ A stockbroker walks into a classroom. His class is ten investors who yearn to get rich. Instantly. Lacking that, they'd like to get some idea of how the stockmarket works. The broker has three newspapers under his arm—all dailies. He begins by saying, "Let's see what the market is going to do tomorrow." He opens the first newspaper and points to the lead story: The possibility of airline reregulation. He moves on to the increased attention that toxic wastes seem to get during an election year. He's working his way through the paper, warning us off of airline stocks, suggesting a few pollution control companies—drawing conclusions, making comments.

The newspapers are the stockbroker's memory model. They trigger ideas in his mind, and the whole thing has a nice, spontaneous feeling to it—like stories clattering off the newswire.

■ John O'Toole, author and one of the most articulate speakers in the communications industry, has a way of doing a tabletop presentation that is extraordinary. It took me a long time to realize how canny it was. He'd come in with a modest sack, an armful from the local pharmacy, supermarket, or hardware store. With no fanfare, he'd start to pull things out of the sack. Invariably, he'd have the leading products in a product category. There could be ten or twelve of them, all different brands. The categories might include shampoo, cigarettes, candy bars, almost any retail item. He'd then discuss (and dissect) the category by displaying the various branded items along the edge of the table, grouping them in a variety of interesting ways—market share, product strengths and weaknesses, "images" projected. Whatever seemed most useful to an understanding of the category. He'd move the items around, enabling his audience to see them in different contexts. It was fascinating—like a game that teaches you something. And it was so simple. The products plucked out of the sack were in effect, a memory model—triggering memories in O'Toole's brain.

Memory insurance, that's what it is. The memory model protects you from leaving something out. It gives you "props" for your memory, and helps the audience to remember what you said.

Here's the nub of it: Try not to use scripts if you can avoid them. They make you sound prerecorded. And they make audiences wonder whose words are being read.

Put pictures, maps, and models in your mind and let them help you make your presentation *unforgettable* for you and your audience.

4

Have you got what it takes to be a superb presenter? A twenty-eight-point checklist.

☐ **D**o you ever wonder what the other person is thinking about while *you're* talking? Do you instinctively put yourself in the other person's situation?

☐ Do you really get a kick out of helping other people solve *their* problems?

☐ Do you use the word "you" more than "I"?

☐ Have you ever watched a debate on TV (or elsewhere) and thought, "That's something I'd like to try"?

☐ While watching TV panel shows, do you sometimes answer the questions before the experts do?

☐ Do you have a good memory?

☐ Do you enjoy "board games" like Monopoly? Do you think you could create one?

☐ Are you sensitive to the sensitivities of other people? (See Chapter 42 for examples.)

☐ When you get into an animated conversation, do you sometimes find yourself taking a *differing* point of view just because you enjoy the argument?

☐ Can you cut through a rambling, foggy conversation—dig out the main point—and *say it* so that everybody understands and *agrees*?

☐ Do you have a high energy level? Do other people seem to be talking slowly to you?

☐ Have you ever listened to your own voice—just to see what you sound like?

☐ Have you ever watched yourself on film or videotape—just to see how you handle yourself, how you move, how you might be perceived?

☐ Is there a bit of cheerleader in you? Do you usually lead the applause?

☐ Do you like to tell people what you've learned? Would you make a good teacher?

☐ Do you think graphically? As you talk, do you see pictures forming in your mind?

☐ If you were to look out the nearest window right now, could you describe what you see in some detail?

☐ Does the prospect of actually trying the exercise in the preceding question appeal to you?

☐ Are you a good editor? Can you digest lots of material into simple, clear language?

☐ Do you like the feeling of being "in control"?

☐ Can you handle pressure without blowing your top? Can you deal with provocative questions without flaring up?

☐ Do you like to show people the work you've done and explain how you did it?

☐ Do you like to demonstrate what you're talking about? Do you tend to "act out" what you're describing?

☐ Are you an optimist? Do you bounce back in a hurry?

☐ Were you in the senior play in high school?

☐ Do you look people in the eye when you *talk* to them?

☐ Do you look people in the eye when *they're* talking to you?

☐ Do people turn to you when it's time for the meeting to be summed up?

If you answered "yes" to at least half of these questions, you're in good shape to become a superb presenter. If you scored less than that, all is not lost. At least you're honest, and *that*—as has been dramatically demonstrated—is clearly the most important requisite of all. We'll also give you an extra point for "tenaciousness" if you'll just hang in there.

PART TWO

The first ninety seconds: They're absolutely crucial.

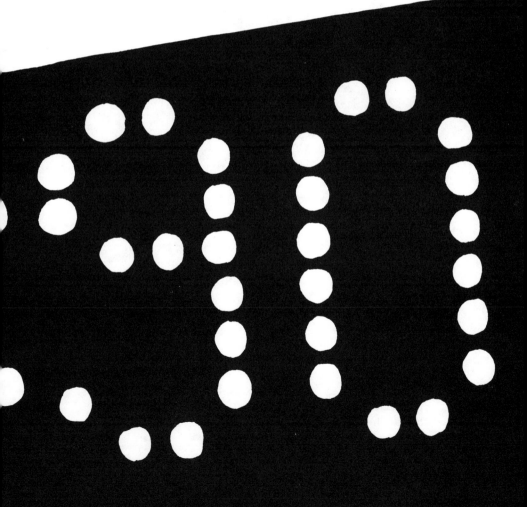

A NUGGET FOR YOUR NEXT PRESENTATION: *"Well, here I am. . . . This is how I turned out."*

This is the presenter. It could be you. It could be me. It could be you or me running for president (actually, it's Paul Simon, senator from Illinois).

It could be Sioux Falls, South Dakota. It could be Santa Monica, California. It could be New York (it is).

The specifics aren't terribly important here. The generality of it is *very* important. It is, in fact, what this book is all about.

The presenter steps forward and opens up. *"Well, here I am, folks. . . . This is how I turned out."*

The presenter doesn't say those words, but the audience begins its judgment of the presenter on the basis of what it sees and hears. The presenter, by the simple fact that he's up there, is saying, "This is me. This is how I talk. This is how I see things. This is how I look. Oh yes, I've got a family and a car and a mortgage—but, in terms of me, *this is it.* You know how people look at babies and say, 'wonder how that little dickens will turn out.' *Well, this is how I turned out."*

This could be your next presentation. Everything is there—just where it always is. The screen is there, in the background, ready to be pulled down for whatever audio/visual aids you have to show. The audience is there, showing its varying attitudes. The man on the far left is skeptical. Look at his face. The man next to him, leaning forward, is interested. There's a man on the right, in a white coat (see him? The one with the glasses?). He could be asleep, but, on closer inspection, he just seems to be slumped into his note-taking. It's an audience of labor union officials, and it's not all male as you'd think on first glance, there's a woman there (behind the guy on the far right in the plaid sport jacket).

And the presenter is there, nicely positioned in the center of things, standing freely and openly, a few notes at his feet, presenting "how he turned out" to this small gathering of people. At the end, they will have an impression of the man—maybe even a judgment.

Anybody who has ever presented to anybody, or even *thought* about making a presentation to anybody, can put himself or herself into this simple, remarkably involving little scene.

What can we learn here, from this situation, that could present *you* to a "live" audience in the near future?

NUGGET: The first ninety seconds of any presentation are crucial. Maybe the audience has never seen you before. The eye is taking snapshots of you, impressions are being registered. It doesn't take long for the mind to react, tune in or tune out (television and instantaneous channel changers have taught us how to do that). As college speech professor Ralph Podrian puts it, "Your audience will scan every personal detail about you for clues to character and temperament." Think back. How many times have you heard someone in an audience say, "I knew in the first couple of minutes it wasn't going to be any good." Or, conversely, "the minute she started, the very first minute, I just knew it was going to be sensational." These aren't impulsive reactions. There's a good rational reason for them: *Presentation is a skill where preparation and attitude are apparent almost instantly.*

Everything you do and say during a presentation will be considered, but the first ninety seconds are crucial.

5

How to get started. It's time for drums and trumpets.

What an exhilarating word, that word, *presenting*. It has timpani in it, and trumpets too. It says—in rich, resonant tones that excite our senses—"Something terrific is about to happen."

"Presenting" introduces the presentation—and here comes the presenter now!

I *think* it's the presenter. *Somebody* has gotten up. Could be a man or woman—it's a man. He seems a bit self-conscious. Never mind. He's thinking about what he's going to say. That's why he's got his head down, and is sort of shuffling along.

Now, he's moved into place—behind the podium, off to one side. He seems isolated. Never mind. Looks like he's almost ready.

He peers out at us. He has that disconnected look of a man who just got off the plane and doesn't know what town he's in.

He fiddles with the microphone. He taps it with his finger. "Does this thing work?" he asks us. Somebody at the back of the room says, "It's okay."

"Thanks," says the presenter. His first words are pleasant but uninspiring.

Housekeeping chores continue. He's got a script—we didn't notice that before. It's as fat as a book. He tidies up his sheath of papers by slapping them into an ominous pile. The microphone picks up all of this rustling and shuffling.

There seems to be something wrong with the lectern light. Off. On. Now he's got it. He straightens his glasses, steadies himself against the podium, and begins.

He's reading.

He's reading into the microphone, and the words rumble through the public address system with the freshness of canned corn.

Is he going to read *the whole thing?*

He is. Without ever moving. He looks up occasionally to see if we're still there.

He reads on—and on. People check their watches. Why does it seem so long since he began? Slides appear on a screen behind him. Why does it seem that he is seeing them for the first time? He keeps looking around, behind him, to see what slide is up. Then back to the script. Another slide. Look around. Back to the script.

After a while, a sort of numbness settles over the audience. After a while, it doesn't *matter* what he's saying. All that matters is when it will be over.

Where *is* this rumbling, mumbling presenter and his hopeless audience? You know where.

This presentation, or one almost identical to it, is happening *right now* in every major corporation, in meeting halls, hotels, and auditoriums from Anchorage to Zanzibar. (A recent article in *Business Week* carried a mind-boggling estimate by a computer company executive. "Thirty-three million presentations, sales meetings, and training classes are held in corporations every day.")

The first law of presenting, if you're a presenter, is to hear those drums and trumpets before you get up to speak. Maybe they're muted, maybe they don't rattle the rafters—but you hear them.

This doesn't mean that you have to roll your eyes or snap your fingers, but it's time to show you know *where* you're going to present, *what* you're going to say, and *how* you're going to do it.

All effective speakers start crisply. You sense that their adrenalin is running high. There's an incandescence about them that you can *see* and *feel* immediately. It's often called "presence."

NYT Pictures

Which one just announced his candidacy for president? Jesse Jackson is a presence wherever he goes—as accomplished in nonverbal presentation as speaking to an audience.

What is this thing called "presence" (and how can you get some)?

■ Presenters with "presence" usually walk briskly, with a sense of purpose. Their attitude is outward, aware of their surroundings—not inward, concerned with their own problems. They project a feeling of *openness*.

■ Nothing is tentative. They don't fuss with things. They demonstrate the importance of their mission by being decisively prepared.

■ They move *into* the audience. (Can you imagine Johnny Carson starting his show in any other way than striding *into* the camera?) They step up to the issues—physically and attitudinally.

■ They project an attitude of positive anticipation. They know what they're getting into *and they like it.* They relish the responsibility of presentation. They create an expectation of leadership.

■ They *look* good. They've gotten "a little bit dressed up"—reflecting their own sense of self-worth, but also complimenting the audience (see Chapter 32).

■ When a speaker has that elusive and largely indefinable quality called "presence," there's no doubt about who's making the presentation. It's something you sort of *feel* if you're in the audience and you *hear* if you're the presenter. (Listen for it. It may be faint, but it's definitely drums and trumpets.)

6

How to "warm up"
an audience without a
Catskills comic or a
Big Ten cheerleader.

There is much to be said for "warming up" an audience.

This simply means to soften the strangeness, defuse the defenses, and slice through the natural reluctance to expose feelings and emotions openly.

Without a "warm up," an audience can be a very cold pool on a gray day.

It's an art to unfrost an audience. It's like an emotional massage, coaxing the face to smile, the senses to respond, the arterial system to open up. Any stand-up comic or Big Ten cheerleader can do it in minutes.

Of course, if you don't happen to have a stable of joke-writers in your entourage—or a squad of cheerleaders—the "warming up" process is going to become your task.

This prompts yet another question.

Who warms *you* up?

The answer sounds impossible, but it's really fairly easy.

You've got to warm yourself up while you're warming up your audience. Before you dismiss that advice as clearly preposterous, keep in mind one small truism which will carry you through many a tough spot in a presentation: *The audience reflects the attitude and manner of the presenter.* Thus, while *you're* getting warmed up, *your* audience won't be more than a few steps behind.

There are two things *you* can do *alone* (that is, *without* cheerleaders or Catskills comics to warm you and your audience) and you can do both of them in those crucial first ninety seconds.

1. *Start by focusing on a friend—one who is committed to your support.* (Spouses, blood relatives, and paid shills don't count.) It must be a legitimate member of the audience who is not a member of your handpicked team. (It just doesn't help very much if you look at your mother and she smiles back at you. Some small modicum of objectivity is necessary.)

If you look over your audience and find that you don't have a single, solitary, legitimate supporter in the whole place, you might as well pick up your easels and chalkboards and head for home. You haven't done your audience analyses, *or* you're talking to the most hostile audience on the face of the earth.

Once you've established contact with your one, true, legitimate friend—*lock in.* Let the eye contact register. Let that person know, by your manner, that he or she is damn important. From that moment on, you and that person have an understanding that is going to develop into a relationship.

> **IMPORTANT:** **Most presenters think that they're just standing up there, in front of the audience, *building a case*. Actually that's half of it. They should be *building a relationship* with every person in the room. And the relationship isn't just for ten minutes, or an hour, or whatever the length of the presentation, it is a relationship that has the potential *to last*—because it is based on a genuine need and an earnest desire to help.**

Once you've made a friend in your audience, you can move on, to another face, lock in, and read the reaction. A steady, open exchange—maybe even a smile or a nod—and you've got another friend.

Your audience is "warming up"—you're doing it by yourself and only seven seconds have gone by.

It's a little like calling the roll—only doing it by eye contact. "Yes, you're here. Thanks for coming." "Yes, you're with me. Good for you." "Are you with me? I'll be back to see how you're doing later on."

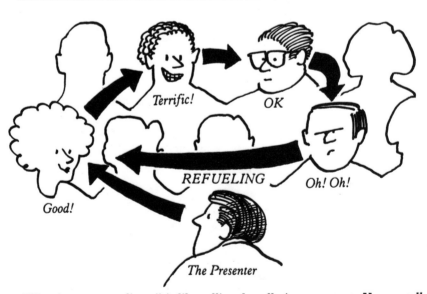

"Warming up an audience" is like calling the roll via eye contact. You can tell who's with you. If you hit a cold fish, don't hesitate to return for refueling.

You've reached a question mark. Face averted. No eye contact. Arms folded. Leaning back and away.

The "warming up" has cooled off. Never mind. You simply go back for a little "refueling." You need reinforcement. Everybody does—especially during those first ninety seconds. So, back you go to a friend, a *known* supporter, and you solidify that relationship—confirming it—and all the while you're gathering strength to continue your quest for more friends. You've got plenty of time. Oodles of it. Only twenty seconds have elapsed and you've got more than a minute to make more friends before your first ninety seconds are gone.

So, refueled and recharged by refreshing a few friendships, you're building more relationships—locking in, "taking roll" with your eyes, changing the atmosphere from frosty to warm, from static to reactive. You can almost feel the climate change.

But, while all of this crucial chemistry is taking place, what are you saying? Is it chatter or solid gold? *What are you saying up there?* Listen.

2. *You're saying something that you really enjoy—that is easy for you to relate—that is relevant.* Maybe it's one line. Or, it could be a favorite quote from a favorite writer. Or, a bit of news that is positive. It doesn't have to be a leg-slapper of a joke, or a feature story for Tom Brokaw. It's *for you,* and the relationship you want to build with your audience. It should not have any hard-to-pronounce words or hard-to-digest theories. It should roll right out of your mouth—without the slightest suggestion of pretentiousness.

Maybe a couple of snapshots will help:

Snapshot: A slender woman in her late twenties gets up to make a presentation to a business group in Cincinnati. She stands there, establishes eye contact, smiles, and says in a soft voice, "who would like to play hookey with me this afternoon?" You can *feel* the audience defrost. People in the audience smile at each other, smile at the presenter, and lean forward. The ice is broken. She *has* them. The warming-up period took all of ten seconds. The chill is off the room, and the presenter is moving gracefully into her presentation. Her subject is perfect for her lead-in: We should use our leisure time more imaginatively, not following the same frazzled routine.

Snapshot: An intense young researcher doesn't look so tense this morning. He's smiling. He gathers his audience and says, "Got an invitation for you. Let's have some tea . . . and celebrate."

The audience is fully awake now. It has been asked to participate in *good news.* Only six seconds have elapsed.

Here comes the tea, right on cue. Everything is perfect. The tea service looks like a spread out of *House Beautiful.* "The tea that you're about to taste," says the research director, savoring the word *taste,* "is our newest instant tea—and it's just been tested in the marketplace. It looks like we've got a winner. Congratulations."

Twenty-one seconds have elapsed. The atmosphere in the room is glowing.

So, as the tea is served, the research director moves into the top-line results of the test. The audience is sipping from the cups of victory, and the numbers *tinkle* with good cheer. Whatever the young research director recommends, chances for approval are now as hot as the tea. *Good news,* coupled with an invitation to *participate* in it, can "warm up" an audience almost instantly.

■

You've seen presenters like this research director, and the woman in Cincinnati. They look into your eyes, say a few words in very simple language, and the atmosphere changes. This is not somebody reading a speech-writer's script or rambling through a few obligatory remarks. There is no pretense.

This is a relationship in the making—friendships forming, real feelings being transmitted. And, always, eyes are making contact.

"Warming up" an audience can be done well within your first ninety seconds. Just start making friends, and talking in a way that comes easily and naturally for you. You'll be warmed up in no time. And audiences are never far behind.

7

An insight from Steve Star: for use within the first ninety seconds.

*I*nsight: *the presenters you really remember, the ones that are embla-zoned in your memory, are the ones that make you feel good about yourself.*

Steve Star flashed into and out of the lives of a group of sophisti-cated marketing experts at the Harvard Business School, and made them feel like blooming *geniuses*. He accomplished this feat during the first ninety seconds that most of us had ever seen him.

Steve H. Star was an instructor at Harvard, a marketing whiz in his early thirties. He was one of those people who *blows* into a room. He rides an accelerating wave of energy, then when it crests—he just sits there, twinkling.

The thing I remember most about Steve Star is how *pleased* he was to have us with him at Harvard. His eyes alone could have illumi-nated the building. But it was his body language that dazzled every-body.

Now, Steve was chunky—with a face that was mostly circular; round cheeks, round chin, plus those great wonderously open eyes. So when I tell you that he *flew* around that amphitheater, roaring up the steps of the aisles, perching momentarily on a desktop, radiating endless energy—like an athlete on a playing field—you'll just have to believe it.

Steve Star was so excited to have us there, to have the oppor-tunity to teach us, he could hardly contain himself. He left words in a breathless trail behind him as he bounced down the aisles and back into the half-circle heart of the amphitheater.

"You know," he said, "the old graybeards here at Harvard are going to be so amazed by what we learn here during the next ten days that they are going to sit up in their graves—slap their foreheads—and say, 'Why didn't *we* think of that?' "

He was on the move again, cavorting through the class like a kid through a candy shop. He seemed to regard us with unmitigated delight.

"You know, I was reading your backgrounds last night and there is such a wealth of *knowledge* here—so much priceless experience—that I can hardly wait to get started. This is just such a rich oppor-tunity for *me*."

He mentioned some of the names and lofty titles of individuals in the class—showering compliments on the room with joyous abandon.

When the first ninety seconds had passed, *the class felt anointed.* There was an air of incredible expectation. Standards of performance had been established, and they were somewhere up around Jupiter and Mars. But, most gratifying, we realized that Steve Star was right!

We *could* astound the graybeards of Harvard—*Steve Star had us so pumped up we could astound the universe*.

Compare Steve Star's first ninety seconds, if you will, with most of the presenters you have seen lately—in classrooms, convention halls, conference rooms, presentation forums.

■ The speaker may be as stiff as stone, looking out over his or her audience with an expression that says, "Well, I'm ready to read."

■ The speaker may not even know who the audience is. (It doesn't really matter because the speech wouldn't change. Politicians are infamous for this.)

■ The speaker may not be able to *see* the audience. Lights can be blinding, and rooms can be darkened. I've noticed that many speakers sort of *squint* when they look out at audiences—almost like they are looking *for* them.

Steve Star creates an impression that great speakers always register with genuine feeling: *they're glad you're there*.

Take just a few lessons from Steve Star:

■ When you're introduced, move into your mission with zeal. Let your energy carry you up there. Plodders and creepers transmit lifeless messages long before they begin. Their manner says, "This is going to be a long, slow ordeal." The picture of a plodder does not generate great anticipation.

■ When you arrive in the presentation area, don't stand there like you've been dropped by a moving van. Move toward your audience. Smile at them. Get those muscles, joints, and arteries loosened up.

■ How many presenters have given you the impression that they're looking forward to the experience of presenting to you? "I've been looking forward to this for a long time . . ." says a lot of good things to an audience. You're prepared. You're confident. You're eager to get into it. Most important, you're enthused about sharing this particular subject with this particular group of people. *Don't be afraid to let them know that you're excited about them.*

■ The place to mention names of people who have favored you with their presence is during the first ninety seconds.

■ *Start*, plunge into your subject within the first ninety seconds. You've demonstrated your feelings about your audience. Now, *plunge in*. Let there be no doubt that the subject has been engaged.

■

Steve Star was aptly named. He's a human meteorite, flashing into the consciousness—*making the audience feel good about itself*. There's not an audience in the world that wants to feel otherwise.

8

Some little questions that can make a big difference in the first ninety seconds.

Sometimes, during those crucial first ninety seconds, you can get things moving your way by asking your audience to help you. Casually. Almost offhandedly.

If you're presenting in a small meeting room—perhaps in a not-so-new hotel conference room—where the audio/visual equipment is a bit antiquated and you never really know what's going to happen next ("Pardon me," the waiter asks, "but is this the meeting that ordered the plum danish and decaf?"), an audience really *can* serve as a kind of volunteer support system.

It's a little tricky, though, so it's best to know what you can ask your audience to do with some reasonable expectation of success and, on the other hand, what can cause confusion, consternation, and delay.

1. *When you ask your audience to get involved with the lighting, you're courting disaster.* "Could somebody please hit the light switch back there. I've got a few transparencies to show up here." Suddenly the room is plunged into inky darkness and the speaker can't find his notes, his slides, the projector, the audience, anything. "No, no—can you bring up the dimmers?" It turns out there are no dimmers. "What about the sidelights, the wall lights?" The well-meaning guy sitting back by the light panel starts throwing switches with reckless abandon. Lights flash on and off in blinding combinations. The chandeliers blink. Spotlights appear from out of nowhere. It's like a Light Show at Atlantic City. The overall effect is not without dazzlement, but it can be rudely disruptive.

The answer is for *you* to have all the lights set exactly where you want them for the showing of your slides. There is a midpoint of illumination where you can see your audience, they can see you, and the slides are clear and bright on the screen. This is a point which the poor devil sitting back by the light panel is unlikely to discover—perhaps in his lifetime.

Unexpected Darkness—A True Story: The most unnerving experience of my speaking career involved the lights in a cavernous auditorium in Dallas, Texas. I had started my presentation on a vast platform that seemed more like a mesa high above the audience. There were only a few hundred hearty souls in an arena that must have seated ten thousand. But I could see them and they could see me—the lighting was just fine. The presentation began. After about three minutes, every light in the auditorium began to dim. It was eerie, like a very slow power failure. As we all descended into darkness, a spotlight of ferocious intensity suddenly attached itself to me. I looked for my audience and saw only blackness beyond the blinding whiteness of the spotlight. Was anybody there? I couldn't see a single solitary person. It was like being alone in an aircraft hangar. But I labored on, good soldier and all that. When the normal lights returned, there were the people—just as I had left them—but I had the strangest feeling about them. *I felt that I hadn't talked to them at all.*

There's a moral to this story: don't let unexpected darkness disconnect you from your audience. If that ever happens to you, throw discretion to the wind and *save* your audience. Just say, "Please bring the lights back up." That's what I should have done.

2. *When you ask questions that relate to the comfort and convenience of your audience, you'd better have the answers.* When you start out by asking your audience, "Is it too cold for you in here?" or "How's the ventilation?"—you're showing your concern. *Good.* Audiences like that. They're people, after all, and they like the idea that you're watching out for them—responsible, in a way, for their welfare. They're already appreciative. But you'd better have a pretty good idea of where to find the building engineer or the superintendent should you receive a rousing chorus of complaints.

I've heard presenters ask, "Is that music in the next room too loud for you?" without having the foggiest idea of what to do about it. (Ask the hotel manager or meeting manager to intercede—you stay out of it. An argument with the presenter in the next room is something you don't really need.)

Show concern, yes, but don't bring up problems that you don't know how to remedy. It's strange, but drawing attention to an unfixable problem will only make it more distracting.

3. *Ask your audience about things that are directly within your control. Demonstrate your concern.* Here's a suggestion for the first ninety seconds of your presentation that's a far better icebreaker than telling a joke—and it will use up much less time:

■ "Can everybody see this chart from where you're sitting? How about the back of the room? . . . What if I move this easel forward a few feet? Is that better?"

Important Note: Of course you checked out the meeting room long before the audience arrived. You've made your decisions on where you want your props and audio/visual gear. What you're doing now is making some slight adjustments to, ostensibly, accommodate your audience. However, you're also accomplishing some other things that can be every bit as important:

—You're showing that you're not paralyzed by your own rigid planning. You're flexible. Nothing is set in stone.

—You're involving them in a nice way. You've hardly started and already *they're* participating, making a meaningful contribution to *your* presentation. That's gratifying for them, and genuinely helpful to you.

The key point: demonstrate your concern authoritatively, not tentatively. You're not worried or fretful about the lights, the mike, the props. You don't want to give that impression. You're starting up a dialogue. You're getting a relationship underway. And just maybe you're also alleviating a bit of your own nervousness.

All that, within the first ninety seconds!

9

"Who's going to be Stanley Kubrick?"

Every presentation needs a Stanley Kubrick. A *director*, that is. Man or woman (Elaine May would have worked just as well in our headline).

What we're saying here is that every presentation needs *somebody* (no codirectors, please) to steer things during rehearsals, to keep things on an even keel during the presentation, to be responsible for the entire effort.

Stanley Kubricks are especially important in *team* presentations. That is, where there's more than one presenter and everybody has the same goal—usually to get something approved. Like a budget, or a strategy, or a schedule, or an acquisition.

When *no one* is officially in charge, *everybody* can be foggy at best and stormy at worst. Rehearsals can be ignored. Time restraints can be flouted. And the various sections of the presentation can become little unconnected islands of opinion. Before you know it, the presentation doesn't really understand what it's about. *It needs a Stanley Kubrick.*

Of course, responsibility also brings accountability—so a Stanley Kubrick whose presentation doesn't get approved probably isn't going to be Stanley Kubrick for very long. Fair's fair.

Could you qualify for the director's chair? Would you make a successful Stanley Kubrick? Sit down right there and scan the requirements:

Job Profile:　　Presentation Director

- Must be authoritative, capable of telling a senior executive or high-ranking officer that his or her part of the presentation must be drastically cut or changed. An unusual level of job security is helpful.
- Must understand that successful presentations answer the *needs* of the audience and are not promotional pulpits for the presenters.
- Must be able to resolve differences of opinion, especially during rehearsals, without causing ruffled feathers.
- Must know how to "cast" a presentation so that the presenters fill their most effective roles. Strengths must be compounded; weaknesses, minimized. It's a little like organizing a repertory company in the theater.
- Must have an up-to-date knowledge of audio/visual aids.
- Must know exactly what the audience is looking for. Should be able to see the world from inside "their boxes" (see Chapter 37).

- Must be willing to insist on rehearsals even when the presenters think they're perfect.
- Must be skilled at compassionate criticism (see Chapter 54).
- Must have considerable motivational ability. Needs to be tough *and* inspiring.
- Must have the guts to call an "audible" when something unexpected happens during the presentation. Doesn't panic under fire.
- Must have the patience to drill his team on the question/answer process (see Chapters 47, 48, 49, 50). Must have the depth of knowledge to handle the unanticipated questions.
- Must be willing to bend the corporate culture, eager to experiment, open to new ways of presenting people, products, and processes. Must be willing to say, "I know we've never done it this way before, but . . ."
- Must have a "grand vision" of the presentation that enables him or her to evaluate all of the "pieces" in terms of a single, desired impression.
- Must be an eternal optimist, able to withstand heavy bombardments and carry on.

If you didn't do quite that well, you can still be a director—of a little different definition.

You see, every single presenter needs help, support, guidance—a kind of *personal* Stanley Kubrick. A manager, time-keeper, A/V expert, critic, and supporter—all helpfully packaged in one person.

This could be you—for a spouse, business associate, brother-in-law, neighbor, or *anybody* preparing a presentation alone. Then, when *you're* working on a presentation and need your own personal Stanley Kubrick, the roles can be reversed—and *you'll* have a solid source of support.

Presentations need Stanley Kubricks—*and* Elaine Mays. They're invaluable. They can make a decisive difference. But, please, only one to a presentation.

PART THREE

Nervousness.
How to tame the fear
that's in us all.

A NUGGET FOR
YOUR NEXT PRESENTATION:
"Knees knocking? Don't tell us."

The hotel ballroom was filled to overflowing. It had been a good year. The employees were bubbling—full of anticipation. Visions of Christmas bonuses filled the air. The chairman of the corporation stood up and quickly introduced the treasurer—who, everybody knew, was to be the bearer of grand financial tidings. The treasurer moved unsteadily downstage. He positioned himself behind the lectern, which was simply a canted shelf on a metal pole, and held on to it for dear life. His first words:

"I'm so nervous this morning. I hope you can't see how badly my knees are shaking."

The reaction was immediate and eminently predictable. Everybody's gaze shifted to his knees and stayed there for the rest of the presentation.

NUGGET: If you're nervous, don't announce it. Once you do, your audience feels obligated to worry about you. Presenters who cause worry don't inspire great confidence.

10

How to get the best out of nervousness— and control the rest.

Show me a person who says, "I never feel the slightest bit nervous when I get up to present," and I will show you a person who is not to be trusted.

That person, no matter how reputable, is *lying*.

Here's the truth of it: some of the world's most famous presenters have freely admitted to nervousness and stage fright—Sir Lawrence Olivier, Helen Hayes, Maureen Stapleton, Luciano Pavarotti, Willard Scott—and many more. You are not alone.

If you're *alive*, your nervous system is going to be going full throttle, or close to it, when you get up to present yourself.

Being nervous is being alive—so how can it be all bad?

It's not.

Contrary to popular belief, nervousness is *good* for you and your presentation—that is, up to a certain point which I have dubbed the Crossover Point.

So, let's explore the *good* side of nervousness.

Positive nervousness activates the adrenalin supply. It makes the eyes shine. It puts an edge on what you're presenting. It generates a respectful attention within your audience (after all, nervousness proves that you think your audience is worth being nervous about). It creates an atmosphere that has a bit of drama in it.

Those are all decent virtues—not to be minimized by hardliners who view nervousness as some kind of paralyzing ogre.

But now we're approaching the Crossover Point. To see it more clearly, settle into this church pew with me on a recent Sunday morning in New York City.

Quiet please, the service is underway. It's a full house and things are moving along smoothly. The scripture has been read. The offering has been collected. The ushers move down the aisles, their collection plates heaped with wads of cash and little, white envelopes.

As the ushers gather at the front of the church, a woman in her mid-fifties climbs the stairs to the altar.

She looks solemn, heavily laden—though she is carrying only a small piece of rumpled paper. She stations herself behind the altar, looking first right and then left as if she were sizing up a dangerous intersection. There is no joy in her manner. Her spirits show no sign of heavenly levitation.

Silence. Then, her voice—small and constricted—tumbles out upon the congregation. She is nervous, obviously, but the words emerge—forming sacred platitudes—and the audience is attentive, even smiling a bit, nodding in appreciation of the woman's valor.

Suddenly, there's a problem. The words aren't coming out right. There are awkward gaps. Meanings fall apart.

Like a car running out of gasoline, the woman's voice is chugging to a standstill. Her throat has become so constricted by nervousness that she is running out of breath.

The congregation shifts uneasily; the minister looks up from his meditation.

We have arrived at the Crossover Point. The audience no longer regards the presenter's nervousness as an endearing life sign but, instead, sees it as a darkening cloud. The nervousness of the presenter has become so worrisome to the audience that it has, in fact, made *the audience nervous*.

Back to the woman at the altar.

She stops. Is she finished? Apparently. The minister moves toward her, reaching for her elbow, whispering a few consoling words in her ear. Steering her gently, he escorts her down the steps and back to her seat in the congregation.

The lady is pale, shaken, but she doesn't realize what she has done for us. She has taken us to the Crossover Point *and* shown us what can happen when nervousness creeps over the line, causing such anguish for the presenter that it spreads to the audience.

Here are some astonishingly simple things the church member could have done, and *you* can do before your next presentation: Louis Nizer, the famed trial lawyer, has nailed the culprit quite emphatically. He says, "A speaker's nervousness or distress is the most communicable disease in the world."

The Reverend Jesse Jackson makes the same point, a tad less dramatically, "I've learned that nervous speakers make people nervous."

First, don't fight it. You don't get anywhere by waging war against nervousness. It'll wear you down. You *accept* it as a positive influence. At the very least, it prevents you from being flat. Then, like Sugar Ray Leonard, you "finesse" your way along—with a lot of technique and no small amount of self-assurance. Keep it positive and joyful. You can *ease* your way through it a lot more effectively than by hammering and pounding.

Second, take a brisk walk. While everybody else is loading up on Danish and crumb cake, take a five-minute walk. That should get you around the block. If you haven't got five minutes, walk around the hallways outside of your meeting room. Walking *before* presenting gets your whole body loosened up (it is *guaranteed* to prevent knees from shaking during crucial presentations). Walking burns off excess nervousness (it is also good for hypertension). It gets you moving forward physically and mentally. It projects you into your presentation in a nonviolent, nonstressed way. You walk in with a glow.

Third, don't sit there with your legs crossed. One of them is liable to go to sleep. It happens frequently. Presenters often get up to speak and find that they sort of lunge forward, one leg functioning and the other, floundering. If you're the next presenter, put both feet on the floor and lean forward. Wiggle your toes. It's okay. No one will know what you're doing and you'll have solid proof that both feet are fully awake and ready to go.

Fourth, while you're sitting there waiting to present, let your arms dangle at your sides. Make believe that your fingers and arms are supported by the carpet. If you can't feel the carpet, just let your arms hang there—detached. Feel the tension draining out of them and onto the carpet. Remember: you're not *fighting* anything. You're just letting it drift away.

Fifth, while your arms are dangling there, twirl your wrists, so that your fingers shake loosely. Athletes do this all the time, usually while waiting on the sidelines, just before entering a game. You're shaking the stress out of them—not violently, *gently.* Coaxing them to ease off, not badgering them. You'll find that all of these sly, little exercises increase the circulation—the blood supply—and anything that improves circulation reduces stress.

Sixth, pretend that you're wearing an overcoat and you can feel it resting on your shoulders. Shoulders "hunch up" when you're cold or nervous. And when your shoulders are tight, the rest of your body feels tense. The gentle pressure of an imagined overcoat will relax your shoulders and encourage the rest of you to do the same.

Seventh, waggle your jaw back and forth three or four times. If you hear your bones grinding, you're probably tense—and the exercise will help you open your mouth. This, to a presenter, is akin to helping a professional quarterback throw the football. Nothing is worse than presenters who suffer from the "tight jaw syndrome." They appear, from time to time, on the "McNeil/Lehrer NewsHour."

Eighth, try that trusty old standby—deep breathing. All you have to remember is this: your breath goes in, your stomach goes out. Inhale, stomach out. (You should feel it against your belt, if you've got one on.) Exhale, stomach in. Do it for *two* minutes. It *ventilates* the body. Before you try this exercise, it helps to have a well-ventilated room.

Ninth, say "Let go." It's a suggestion to yourself, not an order. Tell your brain, your muscles, your nerves, your arterial system *to ease off and let go.* "Let go" will do more to diffuse negative nervousness than any other combination of words in the English language. And nobody can make them work for you as well as you can.

Tenth, don't be self-conscious about having a warm-up routine. Athletes warm up. Opera singers vocalize. Dancers cavort about. Presenters, on the other hand, seem to do a lot of standing around before they perform. *Why is that?* Could it be that speakers don't think of themselves as *doing anything* (how much practice does it take to stand behind a podium?), and therefore feel a little silly doing warm-up exercises? Actually, presentation is enormously demanding on the vocal chords, the nervous system, bodily coordination, and the circulatory system. If those things aren't working, if they're not warmed up and ready to support you, you can be tense, awkward, dreadfully uncomfortable, and thick in the brain. The exercises we've described in this chapter aren't going to make people think you've lost your marbles—chances are, they won't even notice. And if they do, so what? Everybody exercises these days. It's a sign of self-pride and professionalism. Besides, I've never heard a single program chairman say, "Oh my, don't invite *that* speaker. He does funny, little exercises before he begins." Have your own warm-up routine. You'll speak better, feel better, and get more applause.

■

Maybe the woman who lost her voice in New York City will get wind of this book and try some warm-up exercises before she blesses her next offering. If she does, I hope I'm part of her audience. Her voice will fill the chapel and all of those present, heavenly and otherwise, will be mightily pleased.

11

Talk to yourself
before you talk
to them.

One of the *least* nervous people I have ever met is a fellow named Hubert Green—or "Hubie" as most golfing enthusiasts know him. Hubie is a gangling, charming, storytelling, wisecracking golf professional who has made a fortune on the PGA Tour and, in the process, has won the U.S. Open (1977) the PGA Championship (1985), and an imposing list of other titles, including three consecutive tournament wins in 1976. His name is engraved on a lot of trophies.

But there was a time, some twenty years ago, when Hubie was a struggling, no-name rookie on the tour—and to finish a tournament "in the money" was a glorious achievement. His face lit up as he talked about it.

You see, Hubie and I had become partners in a Pro-Am event preceding the Westchester Classic—an annual affair just north of New York City. The pairing was accidental, the luck of the draw, and Hubie had got me. Poor Hubie.

He tried to help me, but my game was absolutely without merit. Realizing that I was going to contribute nothing to the partnership, Hubie really bore down on his game—and I started to study him, figuring maybe I could learn something from this young pro with the deep-set eyes and unusual swing.

The voice was patient, but insistent—like a father talking to a son—repeating the key words, keeping the instruction simple and uncluttered.

Out there on the course, listening to Hubert Green talk to himself, *he was playing by himself.* It was Hubie against the course—blocking everything else out of his mind—concentrating *totally*, telling himself what to do, committing himself to it by *saying it*. It was like he was carving the words on his brain.

Ten or fifteen minutes later, I heard another self-imposed lecture floating across the fairway. It was Hubie again.

> "No, no, no, Hubie. You don't go for pars anymore. Amateurs go for pars. You're a pro now. You go for birdies and eagles. You forget about pars. *Birdies. Eagles.* You're a *pro.*"

His game was improving. He was making some magnificent shots. I was pathetic. But Hubie was carrying our partnership *by himself* to some very good numbers.

In all candor, I didn't learn a lot to help my floundering game, but I learned something significant about presentations, concentration, and nerve control.

> Hubie was talking to himself almost constantly. It
> was as if he was coaching himself, criticizing himself,
> prodding himself. Keeping his mind focused un-
> flinchingly on his game.

Hubie has an unmistakable southern signature to his voice, but
he is very easy to understand—and, outside of the birds chirping,
there isn't a whole lot of noise on a golf course. Listen to Hubie coach
himself:

> "Come on, Hubie, you're a pro now. You don't just
> go for the green—you go for the hole. *The hole,*
> Hubie, you've got to put the ball *in the hole.*"

In fact, Hubie and I won quite a lot of prize money that day—
despite me. I have long suspected that Hubie's most haunting refrain
had quite a lot to do with it:

> "Come on, Hubie. You're not an amateur. You're a
> pro now. A *professional.* Do you know what that
> means? You're a professional. *Play like a pro.*"

Hubert Green had talked himself all of the way around that golf
course—constantly establishing his expectations for himself.

I suspect he has also coached himself into the many champion-
ships he has won in the decades since then.

The same technique works on presentations and your preparation for them.

By talking positively to yourself, screening out distractions,
allowing yourself the quiet luxury of pure concentration, you can
raise your performance level. *You're consciously committing yourself to
your highest expectations.*

Maybe best of all, you can block out the static, the clashing,
crashing pressures that contribute to nervousness.

What will you say to yourself when you're sitting there, waiting
to make your next presentation?

Put your most positive expectations into words and say them to
yourself—out loud or under your breath. You'll know what to say.
Who knows, it might come out something like this:

"I can hardly wait to help these people. I like 'em—
they're good people. This is a great opportunity for
them, and for me. I can make a difference here
today. I can give them something that they can really
use."

NOTE: As you can see, eloquence is not a requirement. But
earnestness is one.

"I've got this subject down cold. I've got a lock on
it. I've studied it, rehearsed it, really thought about
it. I *know* it. *This is mine.*"

"Hey, I know what I look like. I *like* the way I look. I
feel good about myself, my subject, and my
audience. This is gonna' be a great day!"

You say that sounds a little corny?
Tell you the truth, so did Hubie when I first heard him—before
he won over $2 million on the tour.

12

Sometimes,
the best offense is to
let your guard down.

See if this sounds familiar to you. . . .

You're in a conference room of one of the world's great multinational marketing companies. An executive in his early thirties has been asked to identify his most serious weakness as a presenter (he handles some very tough accounts).

"It happens, invariably, when I let my guard down. Suddenly, one of those killer questions comes zinging at me. You know the kind. They hit you on your blind side and cut you off at the knees. When I'm defenseless, I'm vulnerable. I can't afford to risk it. When I get up there in front of a client, I *have to be* on guard. It's a plain and simple case of self-defense."

Suddenly, I had this vision of hundreds of presenters, men and women, standing on stages or platforms with their guards up—fighters in boxing gloves, gunslingers with pistols cocked, gladiators with spears sharpened. They were all *covered, shielded,* protecting themselves.

From what?

From their audiences, you ninny—all those people out there with their killer questions and their bolo knives aimed at the knees (or higher).

"Presenters on Guard" I titled this strange vision before it faded into the very same people with arms folded over chests, fingers slightly clenched, jaw muscles tightening up, neck veins starting to show, bodies back-pedaling—away from the questioner, to the refuge of a table, a podium, *anything.* And, always, the eyes, narrowed—that old "fight or flee" look.

Good grief, what a ghastly portrait, what a terrible, terrifying perception we've allowed to form—maybe even *encouraged.* The audience, attacking. The presenter, tensed, ready to scramble.

From behind his trusty armaments, the presenter says, "I can take anything you can dish out."

"Well, try a little of *this,* " the audience replies, lunging forward with a deadly Kung Fu chop.

It's a Grade B movie, a zany cover for a comic book. Far worse, it's a self-destructing perception for anybody who'd like to win an audience without beating it to death.

I would submit to you that very few presentations end with the audience saying, "Well, that presenter really beat our brains out. He thrashed us good and proper."

A presentation is not a boxing match. It is not a mighty contest to be won by the person who keeps "his dukes up," his battle station barricaded.

Here's a revolutionary idea:

The presenter's best chance to win is by offering his or her knowledge, talent, ideas, wisdom *openly*—in a heartfelt desire to *help* rather than a self-protecting *fear* of being outgunned or sold down the river.

The whole thing is disarmingly simple:

- open up rather than hunker down.
- share what you know rather than guarding what you don't.
- respect your resistance.

Is it too wild an idea to envision yourself standing there with no thought of covering up or ducking away?

Snapshot: Your arms hang loosely at your sides. Your veins are open. Your mind is clear. You're opened up, not clenched up. You're *flowing,* moving effortlessly *into* it, enjoying the tide, not fighting it.

Idea: Let's say you start behind a lectern or podium, acknowledge your introduction, then move out from behind the barrier and closer to your audience. You speak as you move. You have sent a signal. *You feel more comfortable, closer to them.* The relationship has started in an *open* atmosphere.

Idea: You have a script. You glance at it, then put it down and move toward your audience. You may return to your starting point—you may not—but a signal has been sent. *You have moved from a protected position into a more spontaneous one.* You have said, in effect, "Let's just discuss this thing. *Openly,* with nothing between us."

Idea (for wearers of glasses only): You've talked for a few minutes on a formal level. Now, you want to lower that level, to shift into a more personal, "off-the-cuff" manner. You simply reach up and remove your glasses. No big deal. No showy theatrics. Maybe you just hold them there, in one hand. What's happened? You've changed the mood. Such a little thing to do. But, with an almost incidental kind of gesture, you've removed a barrier, lowered your guard. And the audience senses it without being smitten by it.

"Opening up" can be helped along with a few, simple barrier-breaking ideas. But it's mainly a matter of *attitude*—how you feel about yourself and about your audience that day.

If you're confident, feeling good, it's going to be easy. You'll regard every comment, every question, every answer as a way to help your audience. *Everything* in your presentation will be designed to win *without attacking*. To win their votes by offering them the benefit of your brains, energy, or whatever you've got to give. An *unguarded* commitment.

As I say, it's a wild notion.

P.S.: Later, I watched the executive who said that "letting his guard down" was his most troubling weakness. His presentation was carefully controlled, consciously conservative, and utterly bland. He succeeded in not offending anybody. He never let his guard down. Not once. And I still wonder what he is really all about.

13

"Hands never seem to be much of a problem until . . ."

Hands often speak louder than words.

Hands resting on hips during a question/answer session can say, "I don't really like that question. In fact, it's *stupid*. But I'll answer it anyway."

One hand nervously twirling a mustache or lock of hair can say, "Give me a minute, will you? I'll have to think about that one."

Hands in pockets often suggest an admission that the speaker doesn't know what to do with them. NOTE: A celebrated Chicago attorney, C. Barry Montgomery, had thirty-five suits custom tailored with no pants pockets. He didn't want to be tempted.

Hands jangling coins in pockets suggest a kind of Captain Queeg disorder. It can be distracting to an audience, but the jangling speaker seldom hears a thing.

Hands clasped together just above the waistline suggest a rather delicate form of annoyance. Caspar Weinberger, appearing before the Oxford Union—a debating society—held his hands in this way. It didn't do much for his image as Secretary of Defense.

Speakers love to twiddle with their hands. They twiddle with electric cords winding them into coils which are then unwound.

Some things seem to need *shaking*. Chalk is one. For some reason, chalk is invariably *shaken*—like dice.

What's to be done about all this twirling, jangling, twiddling, and shaking?

First, you've got to be aware of what you're doing.

Next presentation you give, tell a friend to do nothing but watch your hands and give you a full report. Or, give the presentation in front of a videotape camera—then see your hands as others see them.

Once you know what you're doing, you'll know what to *stop* doing.

Here's a trick that works.

Stand in front of a full-length mirror with a large book in each hand. Then, *talk*. At times, you'll raise one hand or the other in a gesture even though the books are heavy. Those are the *real* gestures. *Save* them. Eliminate all others. Those are *nervous* gestures.

You'll also discover that the books will tell you *exactly* how your hands should be positioned—bent slightly at the biggest knuckle—comfortably close to your body. Not moving except when there's an important point to be made.

Then, when you get up to speak—visualize yourself in the mirror with the books. Concentrate on it. You'll find that your hands stay where they belong—and you won't twirl, twiddle, or shake again.

14

The world's smallest secret —for presenters who like to stay in touch.

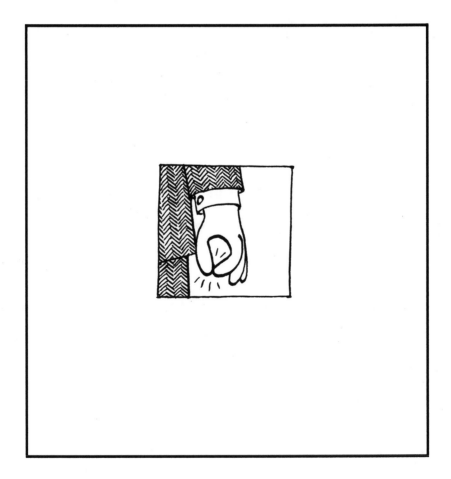

Insight: Presenters like to stay in touch with themselves. Watch them. There are those who will clasp one hand in the other and use them, both hands, like a fig leaf. They will even *walk around* with their hands in this strangely protective position.

Then, there are those who clasp their hands higher up—in a sort of angelic position. Jack Benny used to do this. It finally became one of his trademarks.

I have even seen presenters clasp their hands behind their necks—in a sort of supreme, self-conscious nonchalance.

The Pope can often be seen "looking through the chapel." To do this, you merely put your two hands together, tips of fingers touching each other, and form a "church" or "chapel." Then, you peer through.

Johnny Carson will stand there, looking dapper, with his arms folded—hands clasping upper arms. He's in touch with himself.

Presenters seem to gain confidence or safety, by getting into contact with themselves—generally by doing something with their hands.

The only trouble is, most of these hand mannerisms look awkward after a while. They draw attention to themselves, thereby distracting from more important things such as eyes.

If you are a person who likes to keep in touch, who just feels better by having some tactile reassurance that you are alive, I have the world's smallest secret for you. It is so small, and so secret, that nobody in your audience will know you're doing it.

I don't want to make too much of this because it may sound outrageous to you. On the other hand (so to speak), it could be a lifesaver.

Here's the secret:

Let your hands hang comfortably at your sides (as you're supposed to do), and then touch thumb and forefinger on each hand. Like this:

It has the same effect as hands touching each other (you know you're there), only you don't appear to be self-conscious or nervous. You look perfect. *Marvelous.* You're in touch with yourself—feeling the warmth of your own body heat—but you're the only body who knows it!

15

The night before:
How to get psychologically
prepared.

It's the night before your presentation.

You're presenting to a group of approximately twenty-five people from your regional trade association and everything's all set.

The hotel is booked. Ballroom B, 10:00 A.M., tomorrow.

You've checked everything out (it's an old hotel, but comfortable). The audio/visual equipment works. The lighting seems okay. You've strolled around the ballroom a few times and tried the steps leading to the speaker's platform. (This is important. The steps are usually creaky, and the platform tends to sound like an old attic floor.)

You've worked hard on your presentation. You've analyzed your audience. And you're sitting there, by yourself, at just a little after 7:00 P.M.—the night before. You've got about six waking hours until your presentation. *What are you going to do?*

■ You put your nervous system on "fluid drive." From now on, you're just going to *glide*. Any crashing calamities or "crises"—unless life-risking—will be quietly put aside until after ten o'clock tomorrow. Your mind is reserved for your presentation and your private thoughts about it.

■ Have a quiet dinner, with a quiet person. Nice, but quiet. Don't talk business if you can possibly avoid it. If you're alone, *glide*.

■ If you have made a cassette tape of your presentation, play it by yourself. Just let the words and the thoughts sink in. You're not listening to be critical. You're listening to absorb, to remember.

■ If you haven't made an audio tape of your presentation, take the time to do it. Just "talk it" into the tape. It doesn't have to be perfect. But once you've got that cassette deck in your hand, you'll feel better. You'll know that the presentation *exists*, that it's *tangible*, that there's *substance* to it.

■ Let's hear it now, *and time it*. If the tape runs too long, don't say, "Well, I'll just talk faster tomorrow." It won't work. Edit one self-contained section. You can determine *exactly* how many minutes you're cutting by timing that precise section of the tape. Don't fool around with other sections of your presentation, or trim a word here and a phrase there. Keep the editing clean, simple, surgical. *One chunk*. Excise it, snip it out, and know *for sure* that you'll stop on time.

■ Practice positive self-imagery. As you hear your voice, letting the words sink into your consciousness, see yourself up on the platform in that room. The verbal and the nonverbal begin to blend together, reinforcing each other. Also, you're minimizing the possibility of surprise. You hear what you sound like. You visualize what you look like. And you're already familiar with the environment—so what's to worry about? Relax. *Glide.*

■ The night before is the time for settling into your presentation. It is not the time for massive, unsettling changes.

NOTE: Competitive presentations are infamous for dress rehearsals that are rewritten and restructured into the wee small hours of the morning. Strategies are changed. Presenters are cut. Tempers explode. Audio/visuals are scrapped, costs go crazy. In virtually all cases, the "night before" scrambles are self-defeating. If you are ever caught in one of these madcap affairs, there's a chapter in this book that might pull you out. It's Chapter 46—Your Best Chance to Work a Miracle.

All-night dress rehearsals are usually the result of helter-skelter preparation. "The night before" is a time for confidence building. That's hard to do if you're up until dawn.

■ Go to bed at a reasonable hour—and make a few reasonable resolutions:

1. That you'll give one last listen to your cassette deck while you're getting dressed in the morning.
2. That you'll take a brisk walk before 10:00 A.M.
3. That you'll bound up those creaky steps, take command of that waiting platform, and really *help* that audience.

It's 11:00 P.M. The night before. Lights out. Sleep well. You're going to be terrific.

PART
FOUR

"I'm so boring
I even bore myself!"
How to get
out of the gray.

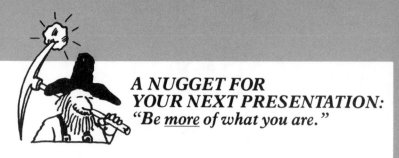

The chart below, which is a classic and has appeared in many textbooks, shows what people say they are most *afraid* of. There were two national studies of the subject—both conducted by R.H. Bruskin Associates, a respected research firm.

The Fears of People	1973	1979
Speaking before a Group	*41*	*39*
Height	32	30
Insects and Bugs	22	20
Financial Problems	22	32
Deep Water	21	19
Sickness	19	22
Death	*19*	*24*
Flying	18	10
Loneliness	14	20

R. H. Bruskin Associates

There are a couple of things you can take away from this chart—both of which are interesting, if not astonishing.

1. *"Speaking before a group"* remains, by far, the most fearsome thing in life—worse than "insects and bugs," even worse than "death." No need to get philosophical on this last point. Research is research. Incidentally, Mr. Bruskin told me there has been no recent updating.

2. While most people relate this chart to nervousness, it fits more interestingly with the subject of *this* chapter—*the problem of presenters being boring.*

NUGGET: Most of us, since childhood, have been told, "Now, don't get up there and do anything foolish." Or, "Now, don't get up there and do anything that might embarrass the family."

We're scared out of our wits! So, when we get up to speak before a group, we become carbon copies of each other. *Boring*. Neutral. *Less* of what we really are, *more* of something safe and conventional.

By emphasizing your strongest strength, *more* of what you really are, you will not only reduce nervousness—you'll be a lot more interesting to everybody.

16

"Podiums are poison.
Lecterns are lethal."

Lecterns have one reason for being: They hold up the speaker's script. Sometimes they also hold up the speaker.

Lecterns have all kinds of bad side effects. They put a barrier between you and your audience when you should be doing everything in your power to clear all obstacles away.

Sometimes, lecterns have "ads" on them. These "ads" may provide the name of the hotel where the meeting is being held (just in case the audience has lost all sense of time and place). Sometimes, lecterns have the name of the sponsoring organization on them. Whatever message the lectern is trying to convey, it is probably not the same as yours. Also, many lecterns come right up to the speaker's Adam's apple. With your head bobbing about on the name of the hotel or sponsoring organization, the effect can be very distracting—if not very disturbing.

Lecterns have another bad habit. They often have tiny tubular lights tucked away under their brows. If you have many hollows in your face, the upward bounce of light can make you look like Frankenstein, Dracula—or worse. Once, when I was presenting behind a rather tall lectern at Ogilvy & Mather, Inc.—a distinguished advertising agency headquartered in New York City—David Ogilvy, the founder, interrrupted me from the back of the room. "Ron," he said, "behind that lectern, you look for all the world like a defrocked Baptist minister."

Of course you can turn off the lectern light. That produces another bad side-effect. *You disappear.* Like a vampire at dawn. Also, if you're counting on the lectern to cast a little light on your script, you probably won't be able to read it in the dark.

That may be a blessing, but not unless your mind is prepared to perform *spontaneously.* If you aren't ready to forge ahead completely on your own, the first signs of panic may begin to creep in. You've seen it happen. The speaker grabs hold of both sides of the lectern, knuckles white, as if it were a lifeboat, slowly taking water.

The best presenters may stand behind the lectern or podium for a few seconds, then—as if freed from it by some cosmic force—move out into a pool of light, probably closer to the audience. This well-thought-out piece of business has some salubrious effects. It says you are more confident of your material than previous speakers who have remained rooted behind the podium. It also suggests a desire to cast aside all foolishness and get down to the nub of it.

Eye contact is much easier to maintain when you aren't locked in place by a dimly lit manuscript, and the whole presentation takes on a different attitude. It becomes more conversational, more personal, less stuffy. Three-by-five-inch cards can be pulled out if you need a few key words to keep you on track. Almost anything is better than standing behind an ad for the local hotel *and reading!*

Now, if you're thinking, "Billy Graham uses a podium," I would only add what Herman Kahn, the brilliant futurist, used to say, "Yes, that's so. But he's got the Bible. Nobody argues with a man carrying the Bible."

Sometimes, a podium is an ad. Sometimes it is placed where it gives the audience ideas—not necessarily good for you.

17

"There's nothing more boring than something that never moves."

I am sitting on the soft grass of Lincoln Park in Chicago watching Alexander Hamilton.

He is standing maybe 200 yards from me, looking north toward Diversey—a singularly uninspiring convergence of roads, bewildering traffic signals, and impatient cars.

Mr. Hamilton is done up rather smartly. He appears to be slathered with gold leaf, and he shimmers in the afternoon sun.

He's impressive all right, but he doesn't move. He's as stationary as most of the cars that cue up on Diversey.

Even though he's dazzling in gold leaf, it must be said that Alexander Hamilton gets pretty dull after you've watched him for a minute or two.

Ever noticed what happens when you're watching something that *never* moves? Your eyes glaze. Ever watched somebody on television who just sits there, or stands there, talking endlessly? Your mind drifts off.

What if Alexander Hamilton, all golden and glittery in the afternoon sun, suddenly turned and motioned for me to take a walk with him through Lincoln Park?

First, I'd suspect I had become an unwitting participant in a TV commercial (probably for a bank). But I wouldn't waste much time thinking about it. I'd want to hear what he had to say. What does he think about Chicago? Any ideas on the traffic flow? And how did he get into that mess with Aaron Burr? Once he moved, *he'd have my undivided attention* (he'd also have a ten-dollar bill from my wallet—and my best ballpoint for his autograph).

But Hamilton, alas, doesn't move. Neither do most presenters—but they don't have as good an excuse as he does.

They stand up in their finery and remain as stationary as statues. They speak, but they don't move.

When a speaker doesn't move, that's really making it difficult for any well-meaning audience to pay wholehearted attention. Static speakers produce listless audiences.

Sitting still, immaculately robed and soberly groomed, may work for Judge Joseph A. Wapner on TV's immensely popular, "The People's Court," but I've noticed that even the judge gets up and rushes out "to chambers" from time to time. Dan Rather, CBS evening news anchor, has also moved away from his news desk—recently, to stand up and move to a relief map of the Persian Gulf (he used a pointer!). Being an anchor doesn't mean you have to be anchored.

The case for *moving* during your presentation can be stated in the most elementary terms.

■ *It proves you're alive.* You are not plugged into the floor. You're not a computer. You are still with us. You, in fact, have an admirable supply of energy. *You're moving.*

■ *It forces your audience to keep their eyes open.* When you move, your audience is obligated to follow the action. Since physiologists tell us that 80 percent of all human motivation is optically stimulated, you'd be silly not to give our eyes a little workout.

■ *When you move, you're reducing your own stress.* Your vital juices are flowing. Psychiatrists tell us that exercise is the best way to control stress. So, you're helping yourself.

■ Also, when you're physically moving from one point to another, you have a legitimate excuse to pause and collect your thoughts. A moment or two not only helps you to get back on track, it gives your audience a momentary "recess." A little silence can be a wonderful thing.

With many of the wireless electronic controls now available, you can forsake the podium and circulate among your audience—lavishing as much attention on the back of the room as you give to the people up front.

This not only keeps everybody involved, it gives you an opportunity to generate a bit of "dynamic tension" throughout the room.

When an authoritative presenter moves into "pockets" of people, tension is created and audiences are likely to stay alert. ("Oh, oh. Is she coming over here? I'd better get with it.")

Staying in touch with an audience, moving among them, interacting, gives everybody a feeling of participation. It keeps the attention level up. *It keeps things moving.*

Those are benefits that don't come easily if you're rooted in one spot, behind a lectern, speaking to people who may be daydreaming in the noonday sun.

You've got a terrific advantage over presenters who are sculpted, taped, filmed, or otherwise reproduced. *You're alive.* So, maybe you think of yourself a little differently. Maybe you see yourself, not as Alexander Hamilton, but as the best traffic cop in your city.

Here's a picture for your self-imagery file:

You, as a presenter, aren't just a stately spokesperson up there, you're a leader—helping people, showing them what to do, where to go, how to get there.

As a presenter, your body begins to move like a traffic cop—pointing to a graph on a videotape slide, showing the intricate workings of a new product, working out an equation on a greenboard, marking up a production schedule, recommending when to "stop" and when to "start."

Presenters who see themselves as traffic cops find themselves moving actively through statements like these:

- "This is the cut-off point. Right here."
- "Look how these two plans compare. Follow me on this, point by point."
- "There are five steps in this resolution. I'm going to show you each one separately."
- "Think of this as a road map, and we've got six months to make the trip."

These comments bring your entire body into play. You use your A/V equipment, you use your audience, and you use your "open aisles" and "walking space" as elements which can motivate and facilitate motion. And you do it without cords and cable that can trip you up, or fluttering scripts that can get in your way.

18

"The audience
is a car, idling.
You are the accelerator."

Think of your audience as a motor car. It is parked, but the ignition is engaged.

The car is idling, ready to go.

Your audience is like that. Sitting there, expectantly, waiting to get going. You are the accelerator.

The audience is waiting to feel your intensity. If your intensity never comes through, the audience will remain exactly where it is—mentally and physically "parked."

Intensity is the personal voltage that a presenter projects. There is a sense of urgency in it, of total concentration. It creates a kind of hush. Audiences respect it.

The question is—*how do you generate it?*

The best way to answer that question is with a demonstration from real life.

The place: a meeting room in a large Oklahoma City hotel. A group of local executives have been meeting there all day. It is now 3:15 in the afternoon and the intensity level is burning low.

A man of about thirty-seven, coat off, sleeves up, tie loosened, moves to the front of the conference room.

He stands there for a moment or two, looking at each person in the room.

"Our city is in decline," he says, finally. "It's hurting. We're hurting."

He walks over to the window, ten or fifteen feet to his right, and pulls back the curtains. The sun streams in.

"Come over here for a second, will you?" He motions for his audience of sixteen people to join him.

"There's downtown," he says. "How many people do you see?" His colleagues gather at the window, peering into the almost deserted corridors of the downtown area.

"Now I want you to look at something else." He walks across the room and opens the curtains on the other side. "Look at this." His tone is soft, nonthreatening, yet unquestionably serious.

The audience follows his lead, gazing into the distance where an elevated highway curls around the city. "That freeway has been under construction for eighteen months—would you believe it?"

Everyone in the room knows it's true.

"I really need your help on this," the presenter says as he moves back into the center of the room. He pulls a flip-chart forward, positioning it close to where the executives are sitting down again. "I'll start the list," he says, "then I'll need your help to finish it."

He picks up a felt-tipped pen and makes a big numeral 1 on the first page of the flip-chart. He scrawls, "Downtown is dead" next to the number. "I think we'll all agree *that's* a problem," he says.

After an equally big numeral 2, he writes "Highways, never finished." He reaches out to his audience, "Who can give me another reason that our city is hurting?"

By now, the audience is no longer "idling." It is charging along with the presenter.

Voices begin to fill the room shouting additions to the list. The presenter writes as fast as he can, rips off the first page and pins it to the wall. He returns to his flip-chart and forms a big numeral 5 at the top of the next sheet. Now he's hurrying to keep up with the suggestions of his audience.

The intensity level in the room has reached a point which few meetings ever achieve. And it's happened in less than ten minutes at the end of a day which, until a few moments ago, was anything but exuberant.

What did our presenter do, in terms of presentation technique, to bring his audience to such a high level of intensity? And how can his success *help you* in your next presentation?

NOTE: There is no way on earth that anybody can pump up your "intensity level" to a meter reading that exceeds your emotional resources, but there are some fundamentals that will help.

■ *Present a subject that you feel intense about.* You can't expect your audience to be enthusiastic about your subject if you feel lukewarm about it. If you're *assigned* a subject, one that bores you, tackle it as a challenge. There must be *something* interesting about it. Find it. Remember—not all attorneys are crazy about their clients.

■ *Start with something that affects everybody.* Intensity usually gathers around a common concern. Begin with a rousing (or sobering) truth. Example: *"Man doesn't die. He kills himself."* (Opening line of a presentation made by Dr. Steven Zifferblatt, a specialist in behavioral sciences.)

■ *Establish eye contact immediately.* This is the fastest way in the world to communicate that you have something of importance to present. It is also, by far, the most intense channel of communication available to you. It creates intensity.

■ *Concentrate.* Probe your subject. Intensity is fueled by concentration. Nothing else really exists for you. Nothing else is more important at that moment in time. Intensity requires an exclusivity of thought, a purity of concentration, that *demands* discipline and practice.

■ *Intensity, yes. Not intimidation.* The art of intensity is knowing when to "back off." You cannot become so involving that you intimidate. There's a fine line there. When you sense that you are "scoring points"—that sensitivities are exposed—it's time to "back off" and allow the intensity to cool.

■ *Let your pacing reflect your sense of urgency.* Intensity that talks in a slow, deliberate manner can degenerate into boredom in short order. A faster pace bespeaks urgency, importance—a more intense attitude.

■ *Get your audience to declare itself, to commit.* The highest level of intensity is active, all-out participation. You will feel the intensity rising as your audience begins to take part in your presentation. (See Chapter 21.)

■

Of course, intensity usually requires a resolution. Passions need an outlet.

A presenter can't just walk away.

Once the car is hurtling down the highway, accelerator pressed flat against the floor, you've got to have a sense of direction. Everybody knows that. (See Chapter 31 for a simple organizational structure, an easy-to-remember guide, that *works.*)

Meanwhile, the ignition is on, the engine is idling, waiting for you.

19
How much firepower is too much?

How *emotional* can you be when you rise up to present your message to an audience?

Recently, in a New York City courtroom, a prosecuting attorney—making his summation to the jury—picked up the bullet-riddled jacket of a man who had been shot by the defendant. With a high sense of drama, the *prosecutor* donned the jacket to make his description of the shooting more vivid. This bit of courtroom melodrama was so electrifying that it prompted an immediate call for mistrial. Despite its visible effect upon the jury, the prosecutor's dramatic use of the jacket didn't work. It may have been perceived as too contrived—too shocking. The defendant was acquitted on all counts except unlawful possession of a firearm. However, other cases involving emotional enactments by attorneys and witnesses have stirred juries and won verdicts.

How soon does histrionics by an imaginative lawyer turn into a melodrama from an old Raymond Burr TV series?

When does the enthusiasm of the presenter dissolve into the snake oil of the pitchman?

To put the matter in its barest bones, how much is *too* much?

The electronic evangelists have done a lot to bring this matter to our attention. They often seem obsessed, driven, seized by forces of such magnitude that they defy belief. The atmosphere can become frenzied, overenergized, a firestorm of emotion.

It's often just a little "too much."

Ease off, guys, you want to say. Back off. Cool down. This thing is getting out of hand.

> O, it offends me to the soul to hear a robustious periwig-
> pated fellow tear a passion to tatters, to very rags, to split
> the ears of the groundlings, who for the most part are
> capable of nothing but inexplicable dumb-shows and
> noise. I would have such a fellow whipped. It out-herods
> Herod. Pray you, avoid it.
>
> Hamlet
> Act 3, Scene 2
> Advice to the players

Of course nobody complained very loudly about these pulpit orators until the charge of corruption crept into the headlines.

Suddenly, emotionalism became suspect.

It wasn't so much a matter of being bombastic as it was a matter of saying one thing and doing another. Those who preach purity and practice sin are inevitably going to find themselves in some kind of credibility gap. And therein resides the answer to the handful of questions posed at the beginning of this chapter.

> **You, the presenter, can be just as emotional as your feelings impel you to be *as long* as there is a solid core of conviction at the center of what you're saying.**

Soaring enthusiasm must have a sturdy base of substance. Fervor, even frenzy, is okay as long as the audience doesn't sense it's all "an act"—a charade artfully crafted to deceive.

Charles Morgan, Jr., one of America's great attorneys, author of "One Man, One Voice," summed up the proper rhetorical style long before electronic evangelism had gone overboard and politicians had made public promises that were contradicted by secret deals. In an interview which he granted me at Muskoda Sands, Canada, in June, 1983—Mr. Morgan said:

> "We are all actors of sorts, some more than others. Lawyers, teachers, preachers. But keep your ego under control and don't let your technique get in the way."

> That struck me as one of the eternal verities of presentation. Keep the ego-inflated pretentiousness out of it, don't let technique alter substance, and you'll be just fine.

20
They call it "chemistry."

Chemistry is one of those words that always makes me a little suspicious.

Let me give you a quote from a recent issue of *AdWeek,* a trade publication in the communications field:

> "It's appropriate that the current review for the $40-million account is boiling down to chemistry. Either agency could handle the business. It's simply a question of the right chemistry."

What does that mean exactly? "Chemistry" has always struck me as a courteous cover-up, an excuse for something, maybe something too ghastly to say in plain language.

Oh, I've heard the delicate definitions: "It's the emotional climate that forms between the presenter and the audience, the degree of rapport."

Well, that's fine. But I remained leery of that word—suspicious that it was some misty euphemism—until I went to Cincinnati and met a man sitting in a hotel ballroom about ten rows back.

He'd been sitting there all day, listening quietly to the workshop I was conducting, and I suddenly realized he had been there for almost five hours without participating—*without, in fact, saying a word.*

So, I invited him to make a presentation to the rest of us—about thirty-five business professionals—confident that we could give him some "compassionate criticism."

"Just speak to us about anything that's important to you, see if you can make it important to us, and give us the first step to take so that we may share your enthusiasm," I told him.

He moved agreeably to the front of the room, settled himself in the center of the platform, and began.

I shall never forget it.

Though the rest of his body hardly moved, his head was like a radar sweep in a dangerous battle zone. It turned as methodically as a rotating summer fan, never stopping, moving in a perfect 180-degree sweep from side to side. His eyes were locked into a level just above the heads of his audience.

His voice carried over us like an announcement in the Atlanta airport transit system. (It had a nice, businesslike quality to it, but you suspect that it might be a computer.)

This fellow wasn't difficult to look at—or listen to. He was quite presentable. He seemed to be about forty, a little on the portly side, slightly balding, dressed conservatively in a dark gray suit and white shirt with a striped tie.

He was talking about the brain, and the voice seemed strangely detached from this small audience in Cincinnati. It's not right brain and left brain, he said, there are no hemispheres. "The brain is a patchwork quilt," he said, "with little patches for sex, memory, conscience, and all of life's major emotions."

The content of his presentation seemed fairly interesting (though it could have been coming from another planet). His head never stopped rotating—his voice never wavered—and his eyes stared steadfastly forward, moving quietly above the crowd. He seemed "programmed," a distant cousin of Max Headroom.

He summed up his presentation ("I don't agree with anything I have heard in this room about the brain") and returned to his seat. There was a courteous riffling of applause.

After allowing a moment or two for the presenter to get himself assembled, I asked the audience for comments.

Silence. No one uttered a sound.

I made a second call for comments—reminding the group that all remarks would be gratefully accepted *as compassionate criticism.*

Still, nothing. The room began to rustle uncomfortably.

Then, from somewhere midway back in the room, there came this voice—male, nervous, tentative—but clear, cutting right through the silence.

"I'm just not sure I'd want to see him again tomorrow."

That was all. Nobody laughed. Nobody gasped. Nobody did anything. But, suddenly, I knew what "chemistry" meant.

Chemistry means, "Do you really want to see that person again tomorrow?"

The second I heard that young man's brave contribution of compassionate criticism, I remembered a phone ringing on my desk several years ago, and a voice on the other end saying, "You know that third presenter in your presentation this morning?" "Yes, sure," I said, recognizing the voice of a new business prospect. "Well," said the voice, "We'd just rather not see that person again." And *that* sounded a lot like "chemistry" to me.

After all of this "lab work" in the mystical realm of "chemistry"—I felt that we owed our speaker, the man who told us about the brain, some honest comments. Here they are, as noted that day:

■ Seek out individuals in your audience to engage with your eyes. Collect friends as you move from person to person. Once you make contact and detect signs of agreement, *smile* and move on.

■ Head movement should be dictated by the individuals in your audience. You move in response to them, *on a personal basis*, not a mechanical rotating system. The presenter is *attracted* into the audience, not overseeing them.

■ There are some presenters who, without ever knowing it, prompt their audiences to think, *"Oh, come off of it."* This usually means the presenter is talking way above the audience—on a kind of elevated intellectual plain. An idea: when you're presenting, look at one person in your audience and say to yourself, "What's *really* going on in her mind?" If you detect distance, or resistance, she is probably thinking, "Oh, come off of it." Ease off. Soften your language. Try not to be so dogmatic. Ask your audience a question. Show that you're sensitive to *their* reaction. You *respect* them.

■ *Let your body demonstrate your enthusiasm for your subject and your interest in your audience.* Move. Draw us a picture of *our* brains if you're talking about brains. What are *our* brains doing as they listen to you? Show us how your "patchwork" theory works. Bring your subject closer to us. Give us a memory test or some other exercise we can do to prove your point. We don't really know what to do about your views—provocative though they may be.

■ *Give another presentation as soon as possible*—within a week. Get used to engaging audiences and drawing them into your subjects. Try offering your knowledge as an inspirational, participatory, exciting presentation rather than an intellectual disagreement.

It's entirely possible that "chemistry" is the most sensitive—and least talked about—subject in presentation. It may also be one of the most important.

21
Participation: powerful, but explosive.

Participate. Make a mark. An X. A ✓. Anything will do *as long as you participate.*

It's easy. Consider these three scenarios and indicate (got your pencil?) which *one* would be most likely to remain in your memory.

The scene is common to all three storylines: *You are in the back seat of a cab riding down a state highway toward Tulsa, Oklahoma.*

■ *Scenario No. 1.* Your cab driver is an amiable sort, chattering away about tornadoes, telling tornado tales that date all the way back to stagecoach days. He's quite a talker. But eventually you arrive at your hotel, pay the driver, and he leaves.

■ *Scenario No. 2.* Same cab. Same driver. Same road. The cabbie is chattering away, only this time he hands you a magazine which shows a tornado spinning across the Oklahoma plains. You study it dutifully and hand it back. The ride proceeds, driver still gabbing until you climb out of the cab at the hotel.

■ *Scenario No. 3.* Your cab driver is chattering away when suddenly a funnel-shaped tornado appears dead ahead. Your cab driver screams, "Hit the floor!" and dives behind the dashboard. You and your cab are lifted off the road and hurled through the air. You land (still inside your cab) fifty feet away. There is a crunching noise, like that of a compactor in a junkyard. The cab driver isn't chattering, but he's alive. He reaches into the back seat and pulls a suitcase off your head. "Damn twisters," he says.

Wasn't too tough, was it?

For most people, *Scenario No. 1* would be quickly forgotten. Reason: the exchange was verbal, passive (and most cab drivers are crummy presenters).

Scenario No. 2 brings a new element to our story—a dramatic picture. The passenger looked at it, albeit briefly, and passed it back to the cabbie. A visual now reinforces the words. By adding a visual (a photo, a drawing, a graph, an exhibit of some kind), you more than double your chances of recall.

Scenario No. 3 is going to be remembered by driver and passenger almost *exactly* as it happened—and, chances are, they will never forget it. *People remember what they participate in.*

It's one thing to be *told*, informed. You're passive. You can take it or leave it. Words are easy to turn off. We retain less than 10 percent of the information we receive (a recent article in *Newsweek* estimates that it's *even less*—1 percent).

It's another thing to be *shown* what you've been told. You're still passive. But the more retentive nonverbal side of your brain has now been engaged. Your chances of remembering what you've been *told and shown* have now approached one out of four. *Much* better—you now have a picture to help you remember the words.

Live presentations have the capacity to confront you with words, pictures, *and active participation*. The possibility of participation *jolts* an audience into attentiveness.

In terms of recording an event or experience in the mind, nothing comes close to active participation. It triggers the senses. It creates a dynamic tension that flashes an immediate signal to everybody in the room—*"You are expected to be ready. You will be asked to contribute. You are going to be acted upon."*

Blood pressures inflate. Pulse rates accelerate. Often, participation brings with it a kind of reverberating *shock* value. Get ready for a tremor:

—A vice president is telling a meeting of managers that precious time and money are being wasted because of the outdated elevator service in a hotel where the company's trainees are being housed. He has calculated the average "wait time" per floor. He has also figured the "trip time" from each floor to the lobby. He has really done his homework, this fellow (his name is David Liemer, an associate creative director in New York). The audience is sitting there, calmly.

He asks them to stand up. He's serious. "Yes, please stand up—I want to show you something." His audience stands. The presenter tells the group that they will now wait for the elevator to arrive at the fifteenth floor. The audience *stands* there, obediently, as the presenter continues. But the atmosphere has changed: The problem has become *real*. The audience is beginning to *feel* it.

More statistics from David Liemer—translating "wait time" into costs. When the "wait time" is finally over (and the elevator has theoretically arrived), the presenter announces the beginning of "trip time." Now, a touch of participatory theater. David has made an audio tape of the actual "elevator music"—that is, the music "piped in" to lessen stress and strain. He plays the tape. It is *awful*. It is scratchy, tinny, awful. Worse, it repeats endlessly—the same tiresome piece of music. There are only a few concluding points to be made now, and the presenter shouts them over the relentless music. "Lobby floor," he hollers, "everybody can sit down." The whole thing has taken less than five minutes, but the audience has a new appreciation of the elevator problem. They have experienced it, participated in it. They can feel it in their legs and hear it resounding in their ears.

NOTE: A few days after the presentation, the elevator system was renovated and the music was put to rest.

Other participatory presentations reside in my mind, one in particular:

—*Michael Colacchio,* a New Yorker who taught a Chicago audience to speak Italian. He was remarkable. Not once did he utter a word of English. He simply *pantomimed* phrases—acting them out— adding the appropriate Italian words, linking them to the action. The audience participated throughout.

"Bartender, give me a drink" was pure pantomime—no English, not a word. Then, as the audience understood the action, the presenter began to make the connection. Speaking nothing but Italian, Colacchio added the words to define the action. *"Barista, mi porte una bevanda."* It became a kind of dramatized chant.

Soon, Colacchio was rushing about the room, pointing to his audience, identifying individuals (by first name, *in Italian*), encouraging participation. The decibel level was soaring as the audience repeated the words. *"Barista, mi porte . . ."* It was pandemonium. Everybody was speaking Italian! Well, *some* Italian. Enough to have a drink in Rome.

Audience participation is the fastest form of teaching—and the most titillating. It may be *the most* titillating at the Harvard Business School. I was there, for a two-week stint, when Professor Martin V. Marshall entered the amphitheater on the first day of the course, gazed around at the forty "students" in his marketing class, and said, *"Well, where do you want to start this thing?"*

The group was astounded. Professor Marshall moved into them, "I mean, how do you feel about it? See anything here that piques your interest?"

The class had been put on notice. The message was clear: "Be ready. You will be asked to contribute."

This is the most familiar and broadly used form of participation.

The presenter *acts upon* the audience. The audience, or someone in it, *reacts.*

■ The congressional committee attacks, probing for answers, "Didn't you realize that you were violating the Boland Amendment?" The witness and his counsel react.

■ "Does everyone agree with that recommendation?" the chairman asks the board. "I'm not so sure," someone replies—and the issue is joined.

■ The presenter needn't be a challenger. "Can you help us out on this, Margaret? What does your experience tell you?" The doctor *eases* the staff toward discovery.

An exploratory interplay begins, and soon the atmosphere is enriched with differing views. There is a cerebral tingle in participation, sharpened by the realization that inevitably, *someone will be next.*

Participation elevates the energy level of the audience (as has been noted before, there's much to be said for an audience that stays awake), but it does something equally important for a good presenter.

Audience participation is a *superb* tool for audience analysis. It keeps feeding information about the audience to the presenter *during the presentation*. The fresh flow of data enables the presenter to personalize the message and make it more useful.

This is powerful stuff, stimulating participation and shaping your presentation accordingly. But, with all of the rewards of participation, there are also a few hazards, and some basic principles that can be crucial.

Here's a short but beefy list that may help you avoid the hazards and apply the basics:

■ *Check the dynamics in the room* before you ask your audience to actively involve themselves in your presentation. Maybe they're competitors and don't want to reveal anything. Maybe they're tired. Maybe they're sporting for a fight (the day-long session has been nothing but bad news—and you're the last presenter). Stand in the back of the room and take a reading of your audience. Listen to them. Check the body language. If the mood is subdued, or the vibes are ominous, don't push your audience to participate.

■ *Make the participation easy for everybody.* Audiences don't want to be threatened. If they're worried about their ability to do what you're suggesting, they probably won't do it. They won't even try. They're not bad sports or anything. They just don't want to look inadequate in front of their friends.

■*Many forms of participation are subtle but effective.* They can even be therapeutic. An example: "Let's take a stretch. Feel free to yawn if you want to."

You'll find more subtle but effective forms of participation *in church* than almost anyplace else.

> "Let's join together for the singing of hymn number 309. Please rise."

"If you don't have a hymnal, maybe your neighbor will share with you."

"Shall we stand for this morning's responsive reading?"

"Can I ask the deacons to please come forward."

Then, as you file out, there's the pastor at the door ready to shake your hand. If you want to see participation being practiced in many gentle but telling ways, go to church.

■ *Involuntary participation can be disastrous.* If you're going to crush an egg in one hand to symbolize the fragility of some organizational structures, make sure it doesn't explode, splattering your audience. (An egg-splotched shirt or blouse can be very distracting.)

If you're going to pound your fist on the conference table for emphasis, make sure the coffee cups don't fly.

Participation shouldn't be an accident.

■ *If you're asking an audience to participate, you'd better be able to lead the drill.* If you're going to guide the group in a memory improvement session, better remember the names of the people in the class. Most forms of audience participation require at least a smattering of talent by the presenter.

■ *There should be a bit of the cheerleader in you.* Audiences are remarkably agreeable, open to suggestion. But it really helps if you're genuinely enthused, a true believer. If your audience senses that you're lukewarm about the whole thing, you really can't expect them to enter into it with much conviction. Audiences reflect the attitudes of presenters, particularly presenters who seek participation.

■ *Don't make one person responsible for the entire audience's participation.* Let me explain. There's always an element of doubt in audience participation. The old friend in the audience, the one person you *knew* would participate, suddenly clams up. "Why *me?*" he says. You back off. You don't rely on one person. Too chancey. "Charley here will carry the melody while the rest of us tap out the beat on the tabletop." What if Charley can't carry a tune in a bucket? Have at least *two* people who can bail you out.

■ *If somebody surprises you and refuses to participate, or tries and can't, just move right along.* No big deal. It may be tempting to say, "Come on, Charley, you can do it if you try"—but participation works best without pressure. With pressure, it can become intimidation. That turns Charley into a martyr and you into a tyrant.

■ *Participation should be fun.* Games make great participatory devices. Short, simple games. Example: *perceptions,* "Let's play perceptions. Let's identify some major corporations in terms of the *Past,* the *Present,* or the *Future.* Tell me, where would you place each of these major corporations without really thinking about them? We're talking about *perceptions* here."

Games should move that fast. The audience is involved, participating, being entertained, without really thinking about it.

■

Nine times out of ten, audiences remember what they participate in. That makes participation a presentation powerhouse. But like most powerhouses, it can blow up if not handled with infinite care and respect.

22

"I'm speaking to what I see in your eyes."

—Mike Vance

Have you ever tried to have a conversation with a cab driver while you're in the back seat and he (or she) is weaving through heavy traffic?

It's very difficult, but it makes a dramatic point about eye contact.

It is virtually impossible to talk to the rear of a person's head. A floundering conversation has little hope of survival without some degree of eye contact. A cabbie talking to a rearview mirror is a miserable presentation technique.

Cab drivers have taught us something else about eye contact. Without it, it's impossible to tell if anybody is *listening*.

In a very real sense, listening isn't done with the ears, it's done with *the eyes*. ("Want to know if a person is listening to your words of wisdom? *Look at his eyes.*")

And as the eyes "listen," they *respond*—sending back more signals than you could stuff into a mainframe computer. Perhaps that is why, Mike Vance—a superb professional speaker—says, "I'm speaking to what I see in your eyes."

This means, "I'm talking directly to the most sensitive and responsive channel of communication in the human system—and I'm editing as I go." That takes lots of experience but it is a skill that great presenters strive to achieve.

Why all this attention to the eyes?

The answer may sound melodramatic (but it's true): the *eyes* communicate a living presence that is indescribably powerful, and no camera in the world can transmit it with the same impact of a live presentation. (You may be looking at Dan Rather. But is he looking at *you*? Are you *sure*?) Live eyes are "the windows of the soul." Doctors peer into them to gauge your health. Lovers stare into them to share their deepest feelings. Hypnotists use them to cast us under a spell. And enemies try to *outstare* each other in order to express their hatred. Eyes are awesome.

The whole subject of eye contact and presentation may boil down to this small sliver of truth:

If you're *not* going to use eye contact in your presentation, you might as well Federal Express your message to the meeting.

Eye contact, if you are *not* employing it effectively, can do more to enhance your presentation skills than any other single improvement you can make. Vocal cords may carry your message, but *eyes* hold your audience.

Since eye contact is so necessary to holding attention, let's spend a few moments answering the questions that seem to crop up most often:

1. *How do you do eye contact? What's the secret?* The secret is not "equal time." It's not a matter of "*three* seconds per person" or "*five* seconds per person" or any preordained length of equal time.

Eye contact is a matter of punctuation. It's the registration of an idea, a phrase, maybe even a single word, during a continuous linking-up of the eyes.

If you're getting a negative response, eyes averted, head turned away, maybe you want to concentrate on this person for a few more thoughts, or phrases, or words—perhaps *something* will strike home. (It is *not* an insult if a person is hesitant to look you in the eye. People don't relinquish their eyes easily—especially to strangers.)

If the eye contact is strong and solid, and the facial language is favorable, you move on—staying with each person as long as your instincts (and your eyes) tell you. You linger long enough to sense an acknowledgment by the person you're talking to. A bond, a linkage, is created in those few seconds and you both know that a highly personal exchange has occurred—and that, implicit in the dialogue, is the message that "you'll be back." The eyes say it all, talking back and forth, an exchange unique to "live" presentation.

Eye contact is doled out by words and thoughts, and measured by body language. But, somewhere near the unfathomable core of it, there is a bonding that is deeply alive and unique to the eyes.

Idea: To feel the depth and power of the eyes, and sneak in a little eye contact training, try this exercise tonight. Find a friend (or lover) and stare into her (his) eyes for *two* uninterrupted minutes. Rules: no laughing, no talking, no touching.

The two-minute continuous current: Can you do it?

2. What prevents eye contact? What are some of the most prevalent mistakes?

■ If you're standing in a pool of light, reading notes or a script, and the audience is bathed in blackness, you're not going to *see* any eyes—let alone make contact. Louis Nizer, the great trial lawyer, is adamant on this point. In his book, *Reflections Without Mirrors*, he says, "The firm rule is: a speech should be delivered without a single note, the speaker looking at his audience in the eye and timing his delivery to match its immediate comprehension." So, Mr. Vance and Mr. Nizer are saying the same thing here, only Mr. Nizer will not tolerate "a single note."

■ If you're just too far away from your audience to see them easily—if you're isolated—eye contact is going to be difficult.

■ "Cocktail Party Eyes" is the presenter's worst affliction. It is derived from all the cocktail parties you've ever attended. There are a variety of "Cocktail Party Eyes," many of which are shared by presenters when speaking to audiences. Here are a few different examples:

"Cocktail Party Eyes"

| "Oh, oh . . . where's she going? Is she leaving with that guy?" | "Frankly, I don't come here often. These aren't my kind of people." | "Where am I? Is this Toledo?" | "Is he going to the bar again?" |

Presenters with "Cocktail Party Eyes" never look directly at their audiences. They look around them, over them, even *through* them. There's a lot of self-consciousness in the presenter with "Cocktail Party Eyes"—but there's very *little* eye contact.

3. "How do I maintain eye contact when I'm really trying to concentrate on my presentation?" Speaking and eye contact aren't two separate actions. With a little experience, you find that one becomes a part of the other. That's really what Mike Vance was saying when he said "I'm speaking to what I see in your eyes." It requires confidence in your knowledge and a reasonable degree of self-esteem. You've got to believe in your ability to help others. As in all aspects of presentation, *preparation* is key. If you're not quite sure of your material, your eye contact will be tentative. Have complete command of your material, and your confidence will come right through your eyes.

■

One other little point that could be important: Think twice before you hand out papers for your audience to study—or give them other inducements to break eye contact. They may get so engrossed in the papers that they never come back to you. And, no matter what they say, people can't read or listen to you at the same time. Eye contact is so valuable. Be wary about giving it away.

23

Spend a day
with your voice.

A voice-over is seldom seen, rarely identified, but can become familiar to millions of Americans.

John Connell is one of those familiar voices. He is hired by advertisers or their agencies to deliver the narration in a TV or radio commercial.

Like many voice-overs, John was formerly an actor on Broadway, worked in radio (he was "Young Doctor Malone"), and started doing commercials on the side. Through it all, his voice has mellowed and deepened, but it has never lost its youthful enthusiasm.

"It all comes out in the voice," John says. "Joy, nervousness, anticipation, authority, boredom. The voice gives the audience its first real clue about you. Yet the voice is often neglected."

Many presenters have never even heard their own voices. At least not as their audiences have heard them. Usually, when the voice is recorded for the first time, the response is incredulous, "Is that *me*? Do I really sound like *that*?"

Idea: spend a day or two with your own voice, and see if you're somebody you would like to listen to.

Simply get yourself a micro-cassette recorder (around sixty dollars at most department stores) and carry it around with you. Talk into it when you're in your car, walking through the park, sitting in your office, or waiting for an elevator. (Nobody will think you're crazy. *Everybody's* wired for *something* these days.)

Tell the recorder how you feel, where you're going, how the weather is. Tell it a joke, if you know one. Describe a movie, a book, a scene you saw on the street. Just talk—about anything that strikes you.

That night, push the "play" button and listen to yourself. Are you somebody you'd like to listen to? How would you describe your voice? Full or thin? Confident or shaky? Personal or distant? Fast or slow?

Describe your voice to your recorder after you have
listened to yourself. Then, make at least three resolutions based upon your analysis. Examples: Pick up
the pacing if you sound tentative (use more verbs).
Eliminate those "you knows" if you have a lot of
verbalized pauses. Speak up if you sound like a
wimp. (This works particularly well in New York
City.)

Then, next day, try your own advice. And listen to yourself
again that night. *You're getting better acquainted with your voice.* You'll
hear things you never heard before. You may notice that you laugh
when you're surprised or self-conscious. You may find that your voice
deepens when you become relaxed. You may detect that you pause
before certain words. You may realize that the words are beginning to
come more easily as you let your thoughts flow into your audio cassette. You may discover that you *like* to talk and that your voice
doesn't sound so bad after all.

Most important, as you become better acquainted
with your voice, you'll find that your "real talk"
starts to reflect the improvements that you've suggested to your tape.

Spend some time with your voice. Other people do. By listening
to yourself, and working on it, you may realize that it not only sounds
better to *you*, it carries more weight with *them*.

24

"Rapture of the deep" can steal defeat from the jaws of victory.

There's nothing like a responsive audience to get the adrenalin going.

Sometimes a speaker can get so intoxicated by the laughs, smiles, chortles, and applause of even a small audience that all sense of time and purpose evaporates in a rising tide of euphoria.

Deep-sea divers encounter the same malaise. It is called "rapture of the deep" and sometimes it ends their diving days.

For a presenter, the rapture of acclaim may continue long afer the audience has expressed itself and is ready to move on. The presenter's adrenalin invariably surges more strongly than the general response of the audience, so it's only natural that the presenter takes longer to normalize or "come out of it."

Hubert Humphrey, the late senator and vice president, was often accused of brilliance that could be beaten into boredom by verbosity. His comments, while smart and insightful, often became interminable. Nothing seemed to stop him, and moderators of talk shows could be heard—behind the senator's insistent, nonstop voice—trying to break in, change the subject, or call for a commercial.

> This problem is not without its humorous aspects, but it can be serious—particularly in "live" gatherings where nobody really wants to tell the invited speaker to "shut up and sit down." Also, in a business presentation, the speaker experiencing "rapture of the deep" may very likely be the most senior officer in the room. It's awkward to tell the chief that he (or she) exceeded the agreed-to time allotment fifteen minutes ago and everybody is getting slightly punchy.

What to do?

If you're on your own, and you don't have someone in the audience to save you from yourself, there are always watches and clocks with beepers, buzzers, and other forms of alarm. Some electronic podiums also have timers. These have merit, and your audience will admire your efforts at self-discipline—providing you stop shortly after the signal flashes, rings, pings, or whatever it does.

There is no humiliation in using mechanical or electronic

reminders of the amount of time that has elapsed. After all, presidential debates have buzzers, politicians who serve on televised panels of inquiry have red lights, and theaters frequently seem to be infested with people whose digital watches sound off at moments of high drama.

You may also want to rehearse your presentation to a shorter time period than you have actually been allowed. If you have been given sixty minutes, for example, rehearse your presentation—under stringent timing—to quit at fifty minutes. That way, if you get swept into the heady currents of ego gratification—you'll still have ten minutes left to pull yourself out of it.

The best way, however, to deal with "rapture of the deep" is to have your own "Stanley Kubrick." That is, a director/critic/time-keeper.

If your "Stanley Kubrick" is imaginative, as all good directors are, he (or she) will come up with a signal to draw your attention to the situation without disrupting you or your audience.

A word of caution:

Don't let your timekeeper make the signal too *sudden* or too *subtle*. Keep in mind that the presenter is deeply into the subject, and feeling a certain intensity bordering on giddiness. If there is a sudden signal—a hand shoots up in the audience, for instance—the presenter is likely to be startled by it, unlikely to remember its prearranged meaning (I have seen presenters react to this kind of signal by calling on the timekeeper, thinking there was a question to be answered). A sudden signal may *shock* the presenter into silence. A subtle one may have lost its well-intended meaning in lingering euphoria.

Here's what your "Stanley Kubrick" can do:

Sit near the back of the room. When the presenter has exceeded the allotted time, "Stanley" stands up and moves to the rear, behind the audience. No big deal. Chances are, the audience doesn't even notice. People stand up all the time.

Maybe you, the presenter, get the signal right away, maybe not. But you'll *begin* to surface. You'll *begin* to be aware of what's happening.

There's "Stanley," after all, standing by himself—*right in your line of sight*. Nothing intimidating about him—but there he is, giving you an expression that says, "Good job. Time to close up."

A sensitive director/critic/timekeeper will allow you to continue bubbling to the surface for a few more minutes.

When it is clear that you should *stop*, that the audience is sagging, your own "Stanley"—still standing, but out of the audience's direct view—will give you the classic signal for "time!" It is pure, nonverbal language.

It may be the quickest, clearest language in the world. It is telegraphic, unmistakable—and it is *hospitable,* not cross and impatient like most broadcast signals. You know the ones.

A finger drawn menacingly across the throat, probably severing the vocal chords. This is unsettling, for the presenter.

Forefinger twirling impatiently in the air, indicating "Hurry up, you're running long." Again, that's rattlesome.

There are other signals, but the discreetness and congeniality of the classic "T" make it the best way to tell a speaker a secret, *"It's time to stop."*

Presenters get rescued from "rapture of the deep" every day—and head happily home realizing that they have snatched victory from what might have been disaster.

And all they need is a little quiet direction from a friend.

25

A true story
about Valium

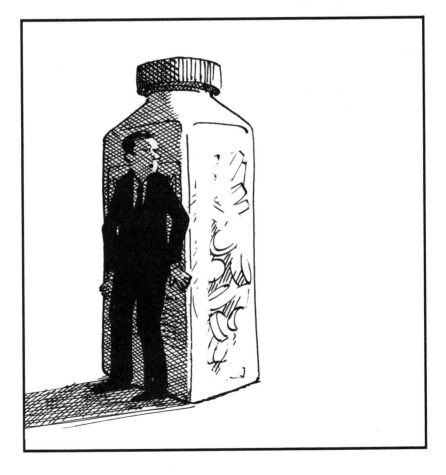

He was a senior partner in a successful corporate consulting firm in New York City. The company was known for its long hours and unrelenting pace.

"I had an experience that could be useful to anyone interested in presentations," he said, "but I'd rather you didn't use my name."

I agreed—and here's what he told me.

"I had a back problem. I also had a speech to give. It was to be in Minneapolis. So, I took Valium through the weekend before going out to Minneapolis. I gave the speech on Tuesday. I was calm. I was cool. In terms of covering the points I wanted to make, it was the best speech I ever gave. Out of the corner of my eye I saw a few people leaving—maybe ten, maybe fifteen. The speech was videotaped and I was eager to see it. I saw it. It was flat. Boring. It was *awful.* I'd covered the points all right, but I was *so* laid-back, nobody got them."

There are two lessons to be learned here:

1. Great content never saved a bad presentation.
2. Anything that makes you feel *un*natural isn't going to help your presentation.

NOTE: Now it's fashionable to swear by beta-blockers (propranolol) as prepresentation stress relievers. These are prescription drugs which reduce the acceleration of the heart. Here's a better idea: Go back and review the chapter titled, "How to get the best out of nervousness—and control the rest." You don't need a prescription to read it, and it won't fool around with your heart.

26

The Electronic Presenter

Electronics has lit up the sky, the screens, and the stages of presentation with a blazing bombardment of high technology.

Live videotape cameras show us the speaker as he or she is speaking—projected, from the rear, onto a giant screen inside the meeting hall.

The live presenter often stands directly in front of the gigantic simultaneous live videocast.

It's awesome. Faces seem carved out of Mount Rushmore. Mustaches become neatly clipped hedges. Tiny tics and twitches become monstrous aberrations. Remote pick-ups often introduce Gulliver-sized images glowering and towering over suddenly shortened live presenters.

Computer-programmed slide projectors are turned on and off by computer, from multitrack audio tape, throwing images on dozens of suspended screens of varying shapes and sizes—round ones, long skinny ones, perfect squares. Multi-channel sound wraps its resonance around us.

Meticulously scripted speeches, or artfully conducted interviews, are now shot on videotape—with original music and special sound edited in. A business executive can see himself or herself at a sales conference on a scale comparable to Clint Eastwood in *Pale Horse, Pale Rider.*

Live speeches, also carefully chiseled out of the intricate language of corporate communications, are punctuated with animated slides and video segments triggered into action by a computer-directed "storyboard." In the process, the presenter can become little more than a conjunction between electronic bedazzlements.

Anything that appears on a computer screen can now be transformed into 35mm slides, transparencies, and "hard copy" sheets. Changes can be made right on the computer console. Electronic "brushes" or light pens can alter images, adding computer-created colors and redirecting shapes, and doing it all in a fraction of the time required by archaic typeset slides.

Many corporate sales conferences are so electronically sophisticated that they would rival a Broadway musical in theatrical splash and splendor. (The British musical "Cats" is an electronic phantasmagoria of computer-choreographed effects.)

Broadway and Hollywood stars—to say nothing of Las Vegas chorus lines—have been known to appear in corporate sales spectaculars. The money is right. A lavish three-day sales conference may cost a company a million dollars to produce.

This is a live videocast on a giant screen. The presenter looms over himself—every tic and twitch magnified for all to see.

The question is: Does any of this high-tech magic have anything to do with your next presentation?

And the answer is: well, *maybe.*

It is unlikely that the next meeting of the Bank Marketing Association is going to feature laser holography or the skating chorus of the Ice Follies.

This is not to pooh-pooh electronic presentation. It's here. Closed circuit television is here. Teleconferencing is here. Factory floors can be transformed into exciting electronic theaters (shows are ingeniously packaged and modulized for speedy set-up and take-down). Electronic character generation is here (large screen format for displaying resolutions, notes, documents). Dolby sound is here. Pre-packaged electronic courses (audio or video cassette tapes, transparencies, games) are here and can be obtained on subjects ranging from "Comic Relief from Seminar Fatigue" to "Coping with Death and Dying."

But, in all truth, for your next presentation, it's likely that a careful selection of *less audacious* electronic aids would be more useful—and certainly less expensive.

Example: With an FM transmitter microphone clipped to your collar (it's no more than two inches wide), you can be heard throughout the hall without having to stand there like a statue talking into a static "stick" microphone. You can move around without needing to shout and without worrying about tripping over a spiderweb of wires. You're wireless.

You can change the computerized slides in your presentation by hitting a button on your electronic lectern (which can look like the flight deck of a 747) or you can ask for a wireless slide changer that lets you shoot out infrared signals that change slides whenever you please.

There are even electronic blackboards now. They don't use chalk. They use felt-tip pens. The board isn't black. It's white, and it takes notes electronically, reproducing whatever you put on the board. Some of these electronic boards will even project your notes, charts, and "buzz words" onto an overhead video screen. Many conference centers can supply them. If you want to buy one, you're talking in the neighborhood of $3500.

Slides, as noted, can exhibit much greater brilliance—with vastly deeper dimension—when produced by computer. Transparencies and "hard copy" can then be reproduced as needed. The time savings are phenomenal. And the costs aren't bad, from $60 to $75 a slide, by computer. If you've got your own computer units, you can knock out a slide for as little as $3.

None of these remarkable little A/V aids will transform you into an "electronic presenter," but they will enrich your presentation and eliminate some of the pesky irritations that have bothered presenters in the past.

When the day dawns that you want to produce, or be part of, a full-scale electronic spectacular—here are a few tips to keep in mind:

■ *The bigger the electronic extravaganza, the smaller the presenter becomes* (unless you're Liza Minnelli). It's hard to compete with laser holography that creates 3-D images which seem to hover in midair. Peter Allen may be able to dance with the Radio City Rockettes as electronic skyrockets burst in the background, but it's hard for the average guy to kick that high. Sooner or later, in most presentations, the speaker must step forward and register a message. Don't let the hullabaloo overshadow you. Don't allow yourself to become a piece of static in an electronic hurricane. There must be a time when you step forward and present yourself as a living, breathing human being.

Let the video segments roll, let the multimedia images explode around you—but don't be intimidated by them. Don't become an usher in your own theater.

Electronic effects introduce presenters, help presenters make their points, but they shouldn't ever overwhelm them. The one unique advantage of a meeting is its irrepressible *aliveness*. The people are *alive*. *You* are alive. That's something you don't want to lose.

■ The more A/V equipment you use in a presentation, the more susceptible you become to electronic goof-ups. Computers are amazing, but they do develop glitches and hitches—they are not foolproof. Unless you can deliver your presentation *without* fancy A/V equipment, don't try it *with* fancy A/V equipment. Never go on the road with a one-of-a-kind prototype system that is guaranteed to dazzle your audience "providing everything goes right." "KISS" is the order of the day. "Keep It Simple, Stupid."

■ Don't even think about an electronic presentation unless you've got an experienced staff of audio/visual experts backing you up *every step of the way.* Electronic presentations require enormous preparation and constant surveillance. Presenters shouldn't operate anything more complicated than slide changers. If you don't believe that, take a look at some of those electronic control panels just behind the presentation theaters. They would frighten a nuclear physicist. Unless you've got a professional staff in the control room, you can be out there in a small pool of light waiting in silence for the multimedia showstopper that never starts.

■ Note from Bill Phillips, New York technician and independent designer of A/V systems for communications companies: "Presenters have a responsibility to be able to communicate to an A/V staff *exactly what* is supposed to happen, and *when*. A/V technicians are not mind-readers nor are they particularly good at ESP." Presenters should present. Technicians, working from clear instructions, should run the show.

■ Lastly, in today's attitudinal climate, it's possible to look *too* polished, *too* slick. Credibility often declines as reliance on A/V aids goes up—especially devices like teleprompters. They may simply prompt your audience to wonder who wrote the script.

■

It's okay to be partially electronic—everybody can use a bit of glitz. But, when all votes are counted and all scores are in, the presenter who is most *alive* will carry the day.

27

Are you Red, Blue, or Gray? (How to find yourself in the presentation spectrum.)

Every presenter in the world operates in one of three zones: the Blue, the Red, or the Gray. There may be some temporary crossovers, zone to zone, and presenters can *change* zones with practice—but you'll find that most presenters are *mostly* Red, Blue, or Gray.

There are variations in the Red Zone (scarlet to pink), and the Blue Zone (midnight to eggshell), but the Gray Zone is one big blob. It is like a Scottish sky when the weather turns ugly.

What we're talking about here is a presentation scale, a sort of color map for your private use in determining what kind of presenter you *are*, what kind you'd *like* to be, and what kind you *should* be.

You can also use this scale to analyze and categorize the presentation techniques of politicians, professors, TV anchorpersons, attorneys, sales people, and whoever else you have in mind. It also works on personalities from history, providing that you have a perception of their presentation style.

First thing to do: Figure out the simple but strange-looking chart below . . .

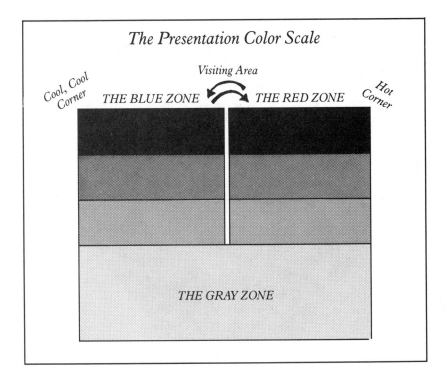

The Presentation Color Scale

Visiting Area

Cool, Cool Corner   THE BLUE ZONE   THE RED ZONE   Hot Corner

THE GRAY ZONE

The Blue Zone Defined:

The Blue Zone is an orderly neighborhood. Things don't get out of hand here. Presentations are disciplined, organized, cohesive.

Here are a few singular descriptives for presenters who headquarter in the Blue Zone:

> Analytical
> Logical
> Pragmatic
> Thoughtful
> Deliberate
> Rational
> Restrained
> Intellectual
> Insightful

The bluest of the Blue Zone presenters can capture your attention with their clear-headed persuasiveness. They can marshall arguments with military precision, and lead you to conclusions of unimpeachable logic.

The best of the Blue Zoners come across as being so secure in their knowledge that they are virtually unshakable. Yet there is an *intensity* about them that builds steadily. They are presenters on a carefully considered mission.

Whether true or not, you get the feeling that they are intellectual. They are most comfortable when speaking from a *very* deep data base.

As you move down the zone, into lighter shades of blue, you'll notice that the presenters change slightly—the intensity fades, the message becomes a bit more diffused, the hard edge becomes a bit dull.

The best Blue Zone presenters *cut through* to the core. This requires a certain sharpness. Not only of word but manner too.

The Red Zone Defined:

Once you're inside the Red Zone, you're going to *feel* it. The atmosphere is charged. If a Red Zone presenter is really up for it, he or she can blow the roof off a sizable meeting hall at any time.

The descriptives come fast and furious:

Emotional
Driven
Surprising
Instinctive
Charismatic
Creative
Impulsive
Daring
Disjointed

Some Red Zone presenters give new meaning to the word "volatile." They push passion to its outer limits. When they have had theatrical training, these presenters radiate a kind of brushfire emotionalism that can be effective with some audiences—disastrous with others.

The Red Zone runs on adrenalin and hutzpah. Its credo is: "Maybe you like us, maybe you don't—but you sure can't ignore us."

As the Red Zone becomes less red and eventually passes into the palest of pinks, you'll find that the presenters seem harder to describe. They become less memorable, less ardent—moving even closer to the most densely populated zone of all, the *Gray Zone*. This is where you'll find the majority of presenters. It is a place that *must* be visited—but not for long.

The Gray Zone Defined:

The Gray Zone is a safe place to be. It has been here for centuries. It doesn't change much. This is very flat country, not much color, and a tendency toward chill.

The Gray Zone lacks the heat of the Red Zone and the incisive edge of the Blue. It survives because a considerable number of people would rather be bland than risk "making a fool of themselves." This fear respects no professional boundaries. It afflicts editors and educators as well as presidents of banks.

Next time you attend a large business conference, ask yourself—just for fun—how many of the speakers you would put into the Gray Zone. The following list will help you identify them:

Cautious
Traditional
Accommodating
Compromising

Predictable
Neutral
Noncommittal
Ambivalent
Boring

The Gray Zone is the absence of color and therein we find its gravest problem. Gray Zone presenters tend to be eminently forgettable. This can be costly. It's hard to win a competitive presentation if the judges have to say, "Refresh my memory. I can't quite place her (or him)."

There's a certain irony at work here. Many inhabitants of the Gray Zone don't know they're living in the Antarctica of presentation styles.

There are two reasons for this:

1. There are so many other Gray Zone presenters that grayness begins to seem normal.

2. Being boring is something that most friends, relatives, and business colleagues don't like to chat about. To bring this whole thing closer to home, when was the last time you walked up to a business partner and said, "You're boring. I've been meaning to tell you this for a long time, but you're one of the most boring presenters that I have ever seen."

This kind of bluntness is rare, and while it has a certain shock value, it doesn't help very much. There must be an easier way. And there is.

To help you place yourself on the Presentation Color Scale, let's get you oriented. Take a look at the next few pages. You'll see some of the better known residents of the Red and Blue Zones, and you'll read a few words about each just to explain, quickly, their various locations on the charts.

Then, we'll get *you* involved.

The Blue Zoners: Some representatives from past and present

The captain of the Blue Zone is Mario Cuomo of New York.

The politically astute Mr. Cuomo has everything a Blue Zone presenter needs. The purest logic. A penetrating intensity. A searching, analytical mind. And a meticulousness about control (he writes his own scripts and reads most of them word for word). Everything comes out "just so." Also, he does not hesitate to leap to the Red Zone to borrow a story, a personal experience. Then, back he comes to the sanctity of the Blue.

Henry Kissinger is right up there with Mr. Cuomo, but further from any hint of emotionalism. His thoughts are carved with a diplomat's infinite care. They move from point to point as if they were being examined under a magnifying glass before being released for consumption. He personifies the rational judgment, the informed decision, the voice of reason. He makes no effort to emotionalize his presentations. He remains aloof, intensely *cool*.

Jeane Kirkpatrick, former U.S. ambassador to the United Nations, shares a certain diplomatic kinship with Kissinger. Both are calm, concerned, deliberate thinkers—but Ms. Kirkpatrick is remarkably direct for a person so sensitive to the nuances of international relations. In an area less deeply blue, you'll find an interesting group of journalists. *Bill Buckley, George Will,* and the dean of them all—*Edward R. Murrow*. They are commentators of an intellectual bent—not terribly concerned with emotional trappings, though Buckley has his moments and Murrow became deeply involved in his stories. Analysts, generally, are programmatically *blue*.

Moving into the lighter shades of Blue, ominously close to the Gray, we find ex-candidate for president *Walter Mondale*. Likable and industrious, Mr. Mondale never registered as persuasive. His story seemed to consist of bits and pieces of logic—and his changing strategies didn't bespeak great confidence.

Should you aim your presentation style toward the heady stratosphere of the Blue Zone?

Before you answer, ponder these points:

■ An effective Blue Zone presentation requires a *ton* of preparation. Be ready for homework.

■ Blue Zone presentations require nimble memories. When questions are asked, they will be reflective of the presentation—probing, pragmatic, seeking more data. You must soak up information and be able to play it back on request.

■ Executives prefer Blue Zone presentations. They feel more comfortable with them. Many executives believe that emotions have no part in business. If you have CEO aspirations, you may want to concentrate on the Blue Zone.

■ Audiences are more patient with Blue Zone presentations. They allow the presenter time to build his (or her) case. Is your personality suited for this kind of pacing? (Keep in mind that Blue Zone presentations must meet timetables, too, and ramblers are not tolerated.)

■ Blue Zone presentations are generally more persuasive than Red Zone presentations—but logic simply isn't as engrossing as emotion. Mario Cuomo may get standing ovations, but *most* Blue Zoners have to settle for polite applause.

■ Nothing wrong with a dash of drama, or a touch of emotion, in a Blue Zone presentation—but the main body of the message must be hammered out of stone.

The Red Zoners: Some representatives from past and present

The Reverend Jesse Jackson, despite an obvious effort to soften his speaking style, is captain of the Red Zone.

Jesse Jackson can be an emotional firestorm. His presentations frequently feed the emotional needs of his audiences, and their responses feed a need in him.

NOTE: Though Reverend Jackson is the quintessential Red Zone speaker, he has no qualms about breezing though the "visiting area" and being intensely Blue for a while. During his address to the 1984 Democratic Party nominating convention, he started his presentation in the Blue, very analytically—with lots of statistics. About halfway through, he shifted into the Red Zone—*and took off.* His audience felt the change, responding to almost every word. It was a tour de force.

The unpredictable *Ed Koch* of New York City is a highly placed resident of the Red Zone. His range of emotions is as broad as any Shakespearean actor's.

If you have ever seen *Leo Buscaglia*, the author and lecturer who is perhaps America's leading advocate of "love," you'd probably put him in the more intense shadings of the Red Zone.

Ronald Reagan is a speaker of such vast experience and vocal textures that he can cross over from one zone to another, but he is certainly more "at home" in the anecdotal warmth of the Red Zone. In the cooler reaches of the Blue Zone, he seems uncertain—a bit frazzled.

Barbara Jordan, ex-congresswoman and now a university professor, is a presenter of engulfing power. Her voice alone gives her an emotional resonance that can control any audience. When she speaks from strong content, which is usually the case, her presentation takes on the characteristics of an incantation.

Emotionalism of a different order is what audiences perceive in television personality *Barbara Walters*. Ms. Walters brings a personal tone to her presentations, but they are always very professional—

sometimes blatantly theatrical. Her style is to explore the sensitivities of others without revealing too much of herself. Nonetheless, she generates a highly emotional atmosphere.

Jimmy Carter projects his feelings, but softly. His voice lacks authority, and the audience worries about him—not much, but enough to cause emotional discomfort.

Let's put down a few additional points to remember as you consider your own presentation style, and which zone is right for you.

■ Red Zone presenters elicit a feeling of participation from the audiences that is more emotional than intellectual. Reactions tend to be visceral.

■ Because their style is more outgoing, more personal, Red Zoners involve their audiences more quickly. Important perceptions are formed on sight. Judgments are also rendered more swiftly. And the judgments are usually clearly drawn. There is seldom much "middle ground" when Red Zone presenters appear.

■ With a Red Zone presenter, content is not the only message. The presenter is an important part of the message.

■ The Red Zone speaker is high risk, high reward. Red Zone speakers make things happen in a hurry.

Now let's see what we can learn down below—in the Gray Zone.

The Gray Zoners:

The Gray Zone engulfs people, swallowing them up in sameness. It's hard to tell one presenter from another, so we won't try to identify anybody. All we really care about is *you.*

Are you in there somewhere? You could be *without knowing it.* Idea: take this quiz and find out. It's not entirely serious—but it could give you some clues:

1. When you give your presentation to your mirror, do you get a little tired of it?
2. Does your particular part of a team presentation often get cut during rehearsal? Do people tell you it's because the entire presentation is running long, and it really has nothing to do with you? *Do you believe them?*
3. When you *do* present, do you find that you don't get many questions after your presentation? *Do you sometimes find that you don't get any questions at all?*
4. During rehearsals, do you find that your colleagues don't pay much attention to you? Do they even leave the room while you're presenting?
5. Do you find that your colleagues give you very general com-

ments about your presentations? Example: "It's a little flat."
Or, "Well, you'll probably be okay when we actually do it."

6. Do you find that a significant number of people peek at their watches while you're presenting?
7. Do you find that the eyelids of people in your audience tend to flutter and fall to "half-mast" while you're presenting?
8. Does it seem to you that there's a lot of rustling, scuffling in the audience, during your presentation?

If you answer "yes" or "well, maybe" to five or more of those questions, you could be sinking slowly into the Gray. Invisibility could be next. Don't chance it. Read on.

NOTE OF THANKS: Much of what you have seen here has been strongly influenced by the research of Richard Vaughn—Corporate Director of Research and Planning at Foote, Cone and Belding Communications, Inc.

28
How to pull yourself out of the Gray Zone

1. **D**emonstrate your proposition. Don't just say it.

■ Lectures are verbal, usually dull. Demonstrations are graphics, usually interesting. Lectures *state* the case. Demonstrations *prove* it.

■ Do what great coaches always do. *Show us* what you mean. Make us *feel* the problem. If you want your audience to take action about the crowded subways, demonstrate how it feels to ride one.

■ Don't *tell* us to get more exercise. Show us three exercises we can do *at our desks today.*

■ If it's easy to learn a foreign language, give us some phrases to *try* on each other *in German.*

■ Your appearance and style should be a demonstration of your proposition. If your subject is "How to Handle Stress"—better be cool. If you're presenting a line of hair care products, *your* hair should look great.

■ Demonstration forces you to get involved. This makes you more interesting to an audience, creates "pictures" in their minds—pictures to remember you by.

■ If your presentation involves a product, show us how to use it. Demonstrate its value.

2. Use audio/visual aids that give you freedom.

■ Some A/V aids are anchors. They make you static, boring, gray.

■ Example: Overhead projectors are widely used. They don't work unless you stand there and feed them transparencies. You become a prop for the projector. Color you gray.

■ If you're going to use a slide projector, ask for a remote control that gives you freedom to move—cordless, if possible.

■ Try using *two* easels—to keep concepts and categories separate and to give you a reason to move.

■ Example: One easel is for objectives, the other is for results. You compare, draw conclusions—referring to both.

■ *Act upon your A/V aids.* They don't control you. You operate upon *them.* If you're using boards or charts, circle key words with a crayon or felt-tip pen. Underline figures, move things around. Make them *work* charts.

■ There's nothing duller, grayer, than one presenter after another standing in the same spot—using the same set. *Change the environment.* Forget the lectern. Move the table. Turn up the lights. Start from a different point. Create your own environment that enables you to move freely.

3. *Improvise* within your knowledge.

■ Nobody improvises in a vacuum.
■ The technique of improvising is based on having compartments in your brain—and every compartment is filled with *terrific* material.
■ Every compartment has a label: recent headlines, personal experiences, funny stories, vivid pictures. Use whatever compartmental categories you want—it's your own mental filing system.
■ Associate each compartment with a visual that helps you remember it. Maybe the "Personal Experience" compartment has a picture of you as a kid—doing something crazy.
■ Let your brain roam freely, scanning those compartments, plucking out whatever serves the point you're trying to make.
■ Keep making connections. Your mind is loose, light, floating. You *know* you'll make another connection; you'll hook up—move ahead—always within your knowledge, always within the parameters of your presentation.
■ Surprise people once in a while. Improvise. Make them think "How did he (or she) ever think of *that?*"

4. Don't break eye contact for more than ten seconds.

■ Think of eye contact as the electric current that keeps audiences turned on. Turn off the current for more than ten seconds and you're going to disconnect the involvement you've generated.
■ Never hand out reading material before you're finished.
■ If you do, your audience will start scanning the material (even if you tell them *not* to). You've lost them. The circuit is broken.
■ *Glance* at your audio/visual aids. Don't study them. They're reminders, triggers—not scripts.
■ As long as you're talking to an audience, maintain eye contact—at least every ten seconds. A disembodied voice, floating over an audience, is no longer in charge. Voice-overs don't get much recognition.
■ If you deliberately give up your eye contact, have a powerful substitute ready. And make sure it gets going without delay. (There's nothing worse than waiting in a dark room for a videotape or film to roll. Continuity suffers, minds wander.)

5. Be more of your strongest strength.

■ Don't imitate anybody. Be more of what you *are*.
■ Take a candid inventory of your strengths as a presenter. What are you *best* at?
■ Acknowledge your weaknesses, but don't dwell on them. They're

probably less noticeable than you think. They may even be strengths.

■ Ask yourself, "How do I want to be perceived by my audiences? What would I like them to say about me after I have made my presentation?" In other words, how would you like to position yourself as a presenter to future audiences?

■ Complete what you have started here. Fill out the presentation analysis in the next chapter. It's short, simple, and can be *extremely* revealing. It's the next step toward getting out of the Gray.

29

Are you the presenter
you *think* you are?
(A self-analysis
to help you find out.)

N ow, the toughest question of all for anybody who has ever had serious aspirations about being a presenter:

If you were going to describe yourself, as a presenter, without undue modesty, what words would you choose? Give us a candid capsule of yourself as the presenter you see in your mind's eye.

Most people, when put in this position for the first time, say something like this:

> "Well, I'd just like to be myself . . . you know . . .
> pretty much the way I am, just me. I'd like to come
> across as being natural."

Fine. You're headed down the right road. The determination to protect your own personality as a presenter can keep you out of more trouble than you can possibly imagine. A few words of explanation as we proceed:

> Starting-out presenters (and a host of seasoned pres-
> enters, too)—lacking a clearly defined style of their
> own—try to adopt someone else's style. More often
> than not, that "someone else" is the *boss.*

This may be flattering to the chief, but it can be disastrous for the rest of the staff—particularly if *everybody* tries to fit into the same presentation mold.

Even if the boss is better than average, the overall impression of a staff presentation will have a certain *déjà vu* quality to it—and if the boss is *mediocre*, there's going to be an understandable reluctance on the part of the staff to rise above that level (especially when everybody seems cut out of the same pattern).

So, hang on to your own hard-won identity. The question now— *what is it?*

The World's Easiest Self-Analysis

There are three things (all short, simple, and self-revealing) that will enable you to clarify your identity as a presenter and help you project it more effectively.

Think of this exercise as the world's easiest self-analysis (at least in presentation terms). Let's just stroll through the three points you'll be asked to examine:

What is your strongest strength as a presenter?
- *How this answer will help you:*
  By writing down your strongest strength, you will give your presentation style *a focus* that will differentiate you from other presenters and still retain what is most natural *to you*. Also, you will find that as your strongest strength begins to assert itself more forcefully, other positive aspects of your presentation identity will emerge.

What is the weakness that you consciously try to block out or eliminate?
- *How this answer will help you:*
  It will define the weakness so that you can address it and cut it down to size. A weakness can fester until it's acknowledged. Write it down; *expose it,* and you'll find "it wasn't such a big deal." Once you get things out in the open, they become much less fearsome.

What would you like your audience to say about you after you have made your presentation?
- *How this answer will help you:*
  It will give you a perception of yourself to *aspire* to. It will encourage you to develop a self-imagery that will feel comfortable to you. And you'll have to think about yourself in terms that your audience might use. That's always good practice.

Before you begin your own self-analysis, scan the quotes on the next couple of pages. You'll see how other presenters handled the same three questions you're about to consider. Names have been deleted for confidentiality, but all quotes are exactly as stated by the presenter.

Examples: *"My strongest strength"*
(Do any of these direct quotes sound like you?)

- "When I'm presenting at my best, I come across with good-natured confidence. There's nothing more exciting for me than communicating with people. I let my feelings show. I figure—why not?"
- "I really know this business. I can answer any question, resolve any issue that may come up. I have total faith in my knowledge."
- "I like the way I look."

- "I can make dry details come to life. I think of them as being alive, changeable, volatile. They're so lively, I have to *catch* them."

Examples: "My weaknesses"
(Do any of these direct quotes sound like you?)

- "I can't edit my own presentations, and I tend to resent it when others do it for me."
- "I blush. I turn beet red."
- "I'm confrontational. I can't help it. I want to score points."
- "I find that I work harder to make the audience like *me* than I do to make them understand and appreciate the *work.*"
- "I'm intimidated by an unresponsive audience. I take on *their* mood."
- "I lose the thread. I'm sailing along, doin' good, then I *unravel.* I don't know where I'm at."

Examples: "Perceptions of me"
(Would you like your *audience to perceive* you *with reactions like these?)*

- "You know, I think that person could really turn our business around."
- "Let's hire her before the competition does."
- "He sees things differently. He would bring us a point of view we've never had here before."
- "She'll take care of us. I trust her. She gives me a good feeling about the whole place. She sets a good tone for it."
- "I got more out of that guy than from anybody else I've heard talk on that subject. He made me realize that what I have long suspected to be true *is* right for me—and it's time I took action on it."

Finished? How to use your self-analysis.

1. *Show your self-analysis to a colleague*—your own "Stanley Kubrick." It should be someone who has seen you make a presentation (either a rehearsal or the real thing). *Here's the crucial issue: Do you see yourself, as a presenter, the way other people see you?* Usually, self-analyses are remarkably close to evaluations by the people in your audience. But not always. Example: If you see yourself as authorita-

Give yourself two minutes a question. Verbalize your thoughts as quickly as you can. Eloquence doesn't count. Candor *does*.

Presenter's Self-Analysis

1. What do you consider to be *your strongest strength,* as a presenter? When you are presenting *most effectively*—what do you think is working hardest for you?

_____

_____

_____

_____

_____

_____

_____

_____

_____

2. What is the *weakness* that you consciously try to block out or eliminate?

_____

_____

_____

_____

_____

_____

_____

_____

_____

_____

_____

_____

3. What would you like your audience to say about you *after* you have
   made your presentation? How do you want to be perceived?

   _____

   _____

   _____

   _____

   _____

   _____

   _____

   _____

   _____

   _____

   _____

tive and your audience sees you as combative, some adjustments—obviously—need to be made.

2. *For your next presentation, emphasize your strongest strength.* If your strongest strength is solid blue logic, be *more* of that. If your strongest strength is anecdotal persuasion, be *more* of that. If your strongest strength is bringing data to life, be *more* of that. Be *the most* of what you do *best.*

Important Possibility: Take yourself *up* the chart, but don't neglect the *possibility* of "just visiting" the Red Zone if you're Blue; the Blue Zone, if you're Red. The important thing is to know where you belong. Once you know *that,* you'll have the confidence to do all kinds of things.

3. *Make sure your weakness isn't really a strength.* "Being different" is often endearing—and memorable. "Being perfect" is often suspect. Is the problem mainly in your mind, or is it really bothersome (ask "Stanley" for the audience's view). Okay, it's a real problem. Here are some real steps to take:

(A) *Confront* it in the mirror, or on a videotape (or an audio tape). Bring it down to its *real* scale. Know what you're dealing with. It's probably *less* than you imagined.

(B) *Apply* some of the *simple* techniques in this book (and others) to control matters. The *simpler,* the better.

(C) *Concentrate* on emphasizing your strongest strength and the weaknesses will diminish or just quietly go away.

4. *Those words you'd like your audience to say about you (the answer to Question #3 on your self-analysis)—run off a dozen copies.* Keep a copy in the file folder of every presentation you make. Read it at least once before every presentation. Pretty soon the words will stick in your mind. You will find that they will help you to *visualize* and *present* yourself as you want to be perceived by your audience.

30

You'll never make an enemy by ending too soon.

Xerox reveals, in all seriousness, that 70 percent of executive time is spent in meetings. What are they *doing* in there?

Most of the time they're looking at presentations.

They don't like doing that.

Analysts of executive time management report that 49 percent of all meeting time is thought to be *wasted*.

This, of course, fits neatly with what Thomas Theobold, chairman and CEO of Continental Illinois Corporation, told me. He says most meetings should start "about halfway through."

In other words, meetings are about twice as long as they ought to be.

This leads one to believe that if you simply started with questions and answers, since they often occupy about half of the total presentation time, you'd come very close to solving the problem.

A few other facts to stick in your presentation plans:

■ Studies show that the typical senior executive can concentrate on a project for only *six minutes* at a stretch because of distractions. That means you'd be well advised to package your presentation "pieces" in six-minute gulps or segments. You'd be surprised at how much you can cover in a tightly structured six-minute presentation.

■ Want more? The Northwestern School of Speech reports that the attention span of an audience is approximately *nine* seconds. If you don't *do* or *say* something that catches and reaches their attention *every nine seconds*, it's daydream time for the folks out front.

■ A recent article in *Business Week* reported on an astonishingly successful company ($45 million in sales last year) in the seltzer water business. It's called the Original New York Seltzer Co. The chief operating officer of the company describes the chairman (Alan Miller) at a presentation:

> "A public relations agency or some kind of firm will come in here with these long presentations. Alan (the CEO) cuts them off two minutes into the speech by simply asking: 'How are you going to increase the market share of this company?'"

Presentations are judged on their management of time just as surely as they are judged on their choice of information. *Shorter pre-*

sentations are a definite trend of the times. Here is an easy rule of thumb.

> Allow your audience five minutes of "reserve time"
> for every thirty minutes of presentation time.
> "Reserve time" can be used for a break—or for end-
> ing a little bit sooner than scheduled. Example: On a
> thirty-minute presentation, close five minutes early.
> Your audience will leave happy. In a sixty-minute
> presentation, you have ten minutes of "reserve
> time." Suggestion: Take a five-minute break and
> end five minutes early. In a ninety-minute presenta-
> tion, you have fifteen minutes of "reserve time" to
> use for the comfort and convenience of your
> audience. And so on, five minutes of every thirty is
> *reserved* for the audience—*to be given back to them in*
> *some way.*

You *take* time from your audience in order to present yourself and your ideas to them. Surprise them by giving a small part of that time back to them—for whatever they want to do.

You'll never make an enemy by giving your audience a nice little gift of time.

PART FIVE

Understanding the audience. How to get inside their heads.

He came rushing toward the platform as if he were running for a train. He reached the speaking area, held up one finger as people do when they've forgotten something and want us to wait for them, trotted back to his seat, picked up a bulging briefcase, and hauled it down to the platform.

He opened it up and started flipping through a vast stack of papers. He was looking for his script. He found it, held up his finger again—and said—"Jerry, do you have my slides?"

A voice from the back of the room said, "Did you give them to me?"

The speaker returned to his seat, and —from some-where—pulled out a drum of slides. He walked briskly to the slide projector, waved his drum and looked for Jerry, "Does anybody here know how to work this thing?"

Jerry emerged from a door (he'd been looking for the slides) and took the drum from the speaker—who returned to the rostrum.

"How's it goin', Jerry?"

The lights went out. A projector came on.

Blank screen. Click. A triangle, drawn by a rather shaky speedball lettering pen, replaced the blankness.

"Hope everybody can see that," the speaker said, still puttering, "because you're going to be lookin' at it for the next thirty minutes."

Behind me, I heard a loud whisper say, "Think I'll head for the bar."

NUGGET: An ill-prepared presenter sends a dramatic message to his or her audience: "I don't think you're very important. If you were, I'd be better prepared." Audiences are sensitive. They pick up signals and react to them personally.

31

A simple structure
for your next presentation.
It's "All About Them."

Is there anyone anywhere who hasn't been forced to write a "speech outline" or a "thesis outline" or some other kind of outline following this nervous contour?

I.
    A.
    B.
        1.
        2.
        3.
            a.
            b.
            c.
        4.
    C.
    D.
II.

Outlines can frazzle your brain. Should "History of Manchuria" be a big A or a little a?

Most of the outlines I've seen have all of the appeal of a sleepless night. They look like very long grocery lists, with each item somehow rated by how far it's indented.

Outlines can be so boring to write that professional speechwriters often write the outline *after* the script. It's true. It's a bit like bombing the harbor and then writing the strategy (just in case anyone should ask).

Also, a complicated, cumbersome outline simply cannot be remembered. An outline should help you remember the path of your presentation. It should lend itself to graphic interpretation—so that you can make a map of it.

Your presentation structure, to be of any use whatsoever, must be simple enough to be remembered. It must be simple enough so that *you'll* remember what you want to say, and *your audience* will have no difficulty remembering what you told them.

John S. Wood, Commercial Attaché at the United States Embassy in Mexico City, is a tall, imposing presenter who uses a speech structure that is classic in its simplicity.

I asked him to draw me a picture of the structure he uses. He said "gladly" and scribbled this sketch on his paper napkin (he did the whole thing in about twenty seconds).

JOKES, STORIES, ANECDOTES

Tell them what you're going to tell them.

JOKES, STORIES, ANECDOTES

Tell them.

JOKES, STORIES, ANECDOTES

Tell them what you told them.

John Wood, it should be noted, is a superb storyteller (dialects, imitations, everything). And a tall, funny man from the U.S. Department of Commerce is a stellar attraction on the foreign service speaking circuit. John makes a presentation every other week. It is based on simplicity of structure, sturdy content, sandwiched with humor. You can't do much better.

In point of fact, the John Wood speech structure is a personalized variation of what has been fundamental to the subject since the time of Cicero.

    I. The Opening
   II. The Core
  III. The Close

There are literally thousands of extensions and elaborations of that basic three-point structure, but—after reviewing dozens of them—I realized that John Wood's outline was surely the simplest, if not the best, and all the others would grind this chapter to an overloaded halt.

However, with all due respect to John, I did think that *Cicero* might be worth noting.

He wrote the first handbook for orators (somewhere around 100 B.C.) and his reputation as a speaker/orator has endured for over twenty centuries. That says something for his immortality. He was no slouch at defining structures either.

Here from a little crimson book called (Cicero) *Ad Herennium (Book I),* "On the Theory of Public Speaking"—are Cicero's rules of discourse:

Cicero's Six Rules of Discourse

I. Introduction ("get attention").

II. Statement of Facts (background). Emphasis on brevity, clarity, plausibility.

III. Division (areas of agreement, disagreement, decisions needed).

IV. Proof (positions on pending matters—with supporting evidence).

V. Refutation ("destruction of our adversaries' arguments," Cicero was tough as nails).

VI. Conclusion (the end "formed in the accordance of art"). This meant, I assume, to remind your audience of its responsibility in the matters at hand and leave gracefully.

Should anyone wish to summarize, Sections I, II, and III could be called:

■ *Understanding the Problem*

Sections IV and V could be:

■ *Resolving the Problem (competitively)*

And Section VI could be:

■ *Taking Action (gracefully).*

Cicero, incidentally, sounds pretty stern in his rules of discourse—but scan the rest of his theories on public speaking, and you get the feeling that he would endorse John Wood's structure, particularly the emphasis on "jokes, stories, and anecdotes." Listen to this, from Cicero's pen:

"If the hearers have been fatigued by listening, we shall open with something that provides laughter—a fable, a plausible fiction, a caricature, an ironical inversion of the meaning of a word, an ambiguity, innuendo, banter, a pun . . . a challenge or a smile of approbation directed at someone."

Cicero understood audiences, didn't he? *Wake them up,* he says. Tell a story. Banter. Pun. Smile. *Do something!*

Back there, in the dusty courtyards and bustling halls of Rome, it seems only natural that there would be lively conversations around heavy tables—leading directly to presentations of one kind or another.

"You know, there's an issue here that troubles me. It troubles me greatly, and we seem unable to deal with it."

It could be about anything. Politics. Law. Education.

"We were wondering if you could give us your point of view. Tell us how you see it."

The attention centers on one person in the group.

"Of course we'd want to know why you think as you do."

The person singled out now realizes that something must be said, some response.

"Then, if you have an idea, a proposal, we'd be glad to hear it."

And so, perhaps, the presentation begins—just as it does over thirty million times *every day* throughout the U.S.

The situation suggests a graphic structure that could be appropriate for your next presentation.

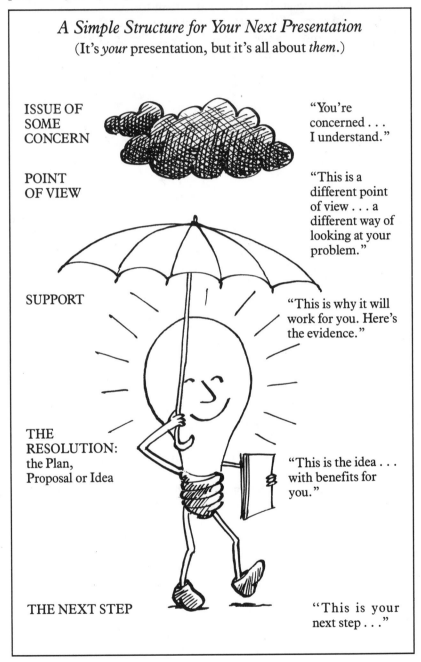

A Simple Structure for Your Next Presentation
(It's *your* presentation, but it's all about *them*.)

ISSUE OF
SOME
CONCERN

"You're
concerned . . .
I understand."

POINT
OF VIEW

"This is a
different point
of view . . . a
different way of
looking at your
problem."

SUPPORT

"This is why it will
work for you. Here's
the evidence."

THE
RESOLUTION:
the Plan,
Proposal or Idea

"This is the idea . . .
with benefits for
you."

THE NEXT STEP

"This is your
next step . . ."

Every part and parcel of that presentation concerns the audience. It *starts* with an issue of concern to the audience, and *ends* with "the next step" towards resolution of the issue. From start to finish the presenter is the guide—presenting his or her views, data, plans, ideas, processes—*but always talking in their (the audience's) terms.* Audiences invariably believe the best presentations are *all about them.*

The "All About Them" Presentation Structure

- *Start* with an issue of direct concern to the audience (it could also be an opportunity).
- *Provide* them with a different point of view, a different way of looking at *their* problem.
- *Back it up* with evidence.
- *Offer* a resolution (an idea!). Could be a proposal, plan, package, product. Mention the benefits.
- *Suggest* the next step to take. It should be as specific as possible.

The structure, "All About Them," may sound like a lot of homework for *you*. Not as much as you might suppose. Presentations do require audience analysis, and digging. But what you are really doing is applying your *knowledge strategically,* so that every bit of it relates directly to the self-interest of your audience.

"All About Them" can be used on any subject for any audience, because all audiences—probably even back in Cicero's day—are sitting there wondering, *"When is the presenter going to start talking about me?"*

32

What to wear
to a winning presentation
(when you're the presenter).

What you wear, when making a presentation, is one of the strongest components of what you communicate.

Here's why:

■ Your clothes—or, more specifically, what you choose to wear—are pure, *nonverbal* communication. Clothes communicate almost instantaneously, as quickly as the eye can telegraph a snapshot to the mind.

■ Clothes provide a self-portrait of *you*. You are what you wear. Fashion has drummed this concept into our minds—and it has achieved a certain credibility.

■ Clothes are universal. Everybody wears them. Outside of a nudist camp, you won't find many audiences totally disregarding the importance of clothes.

Thus, you can't dismiss or pooh-pooh the relevance of clothes to your presentation effectiveness. They're *very* important.

What you wear tells us, your audience, two fundamental things:

—your perception of *yourself,*
—your perception of *us.*

Let's start with you:

For most people, clothes are a deliberate indication of lifestyle and attitude. Shirts and blouses speak volumes. Colors make announcements, sometimes loud and raucous—sometimes shy and muted.

Shoes talk. Wingtips say one thing; sandals, another. Scarves, jewelry, eyeglasses—they all make their own presentations of your taste and personality.

How do you see yourself? Your clothes give us, your audience, our very first clue. Your clothes communicate your aspirations for yourself. Unless you are standing behind a podium that covers up everything except your head, your audience is going to notice your clothes.

After all, you're *presenting* yourself—and clothes are part of the portrait.

Many presenters don't consciously think about what they're wearing—and that comes across, too. Color them gray, rumpled, diffident, unconcerned with the vagaries of passing fashion.

Here's the point: whether accurate or faulty, perceptions are going to be made—and your clothes will contribute.

You don't want to give your audience the wrong perception before you've even spoken a word.

Your style of dress should be an extension of your strongest strength.

Example: If you're a designer or interior decorator, why not show us your understanding of color and texture by the way you dress? Dress can be a demonstration of special talents as well as a projection of a special personality.

Another example, more subtle: If you're an analyst or financial consultant, why not wear an outfit that is nicely coordinated—that comes together naturally—just as the pieces of a deal or transaction fit together in you mind?

Will your audience make this subtle connection, or is it *too* subtle, *too* subliminal? Even if most of your audience doesn't make the precise connection between a well-coordinated outfit and a well-ordered mind, they'll see you as successful—and that's not half-bad. Audiences relate success to dress.

There is absolutely nothing wrong in selecting clothes that strengthen the perception that you want to project. *Who says that presenters must blend into the woodwork?*

Before we go any further with this, there's something you should know about audiences:

Most audiences tend to be suspicious of presenters who show up in unfamiliar garb.

If you're not known for your unique wardrobe, it's not wise to appear on the scene in black leather and heavy metal.

If you're not Willie Nelson, you're probably well advised to leave your headband at home and get a haircut (or at least a trim). If you're not Joan Collins, beware of cleavage. Celebrities can be a bit scandalous (it's expected), but strangers in strange outfits are simply regarded as oddities.

Let's see if we can construct a rule for at least *most* of the time:

Dress in a manner that projects your strongest strength, but don't *shock* your audience (unless you're famous and people love you for your eccentricities). As John Wood of the U.S. Department of Commerce says, "You must blend in with your audience, but you must also be memorable."

Another thing (perhaps the most important thing): you should be comfortable. You should feel good about what you're wearing.

NOTE: Disregard all of those courtroom dramas you've seen. You know the ones I mean. Courtroom attorneys seem to think that a subway mugger poured into a pinstriped suit will register on the jury as a pillar of the community. A mugger in a Wall Street suit invariably looks like nothing more than a very uncomfortable mugger.

Don't dress to project a personality that isn't yours. You'll just be miserable.

A few other tips to improve how the audience perceives you:

1. Take the stuff out of your pockets that make them look stuffed. The eyeglasses, the wadded-up handkerchief, the airplane ticket to Phoenix, the grocery list, the taxi receipts, the notepad from the hotel, *all that stuff.*

2. Remove the objects from your clothes that make noise. The coins that jangle. The pills that clatter in their little plastic vial. The keys on their chain. Some presenters walk across a stage or platform and sound like a pick-up truck from the Salvation Army. Your clothes can create *audio* impressions as well as video.

3. Some presenters use their clothes as "props." A tie loosened at the collar, a coat removed and tossed across a chair—such touches of theatrical business can communicate intensity, informality, a shirt-sleeves approach.

A woman, hands in pockets of a very chic designer outfit, can register poise, sophistication, thoughtfulness.

Using what you wear to help create desired perceptions is simply utilizing one of your best means of communications.

Clothes don't just cover, they *communicate.* They don't just protect you, they project you. They present your perception of yourself.

What about the other half of the equation? What about *your* perception of *them*—the people out there in your audience? What do your clothes say about *them?*

The answer is short and simple. It is so unsophisticated that it probably predates the invention of fashion.

We tend to like people who, on special occasions, get a little bit dressed up for us. Nothing splashy. Nothing flashy. "Just a little bit" dressed up.

Your presentation to any audience is one of those special occasions. By dressing up a notch, by dressing appropriately but with obvious care—you're showing your audience that you think *they are important.*

They look at you and they *see* that you want to make a good impression. That's a nice form of flattery. Presenters aren't the only people who appreciate a little praise.

NOTE: When someone in your audience peers at you and whispers, "Hey, that must be the speaker," you've probably dressed just right.

Now, nobody's expecting you to rush out to Gucci's and spend a fortune before your next speaking engagement—or put your paycheck into a lush new wardrobe—but it certainly won't hurt you to wear your nicest, most becoming sports outfit to a presentation you're going to make at LaCosta, the Greenbrier, or the local country club.

It certainly won't hurt you to wear your newest, best fitting business suit to that executive staff meeting you've been asked to brief.

Compliment your audience by what you wear. Let your clothes communicate that you think your audience is important. Yes, you got "a little bit dressed" up—and you hope it shows. After all, *they're worth it.*

That's a perception that any self-respecting audience will applaud.

33

Palaver:
Is it helpful, harmful, or just hot air?

It's fashionable to be *anti-meeting* these days. Most people tend to think there are too many meetings, or they last too long, or they're badly handled. All of which has considerable merit, but there seems to be one part of most meetings which is seldom, if ever, criticized.

Let's call it the *palaver* section.

There's *harmless* palaver.

—"Boy, are we ever glad to be here today and have this chance to get acquainted. We have admired your company for so long . . . and we have so many things in common that . . ." Palaver, palaver.

—"Did you see that football game on TV yesterday? Wasn't that some kind of game? How 'bout that last quarter?"

Then, there's the weather, the traffic, the weekend. It's all harmless palaver that may, in fact, be useful in some localities. It's just part of the culture.

> **Self-conscious palaver is something else. It doesn't serve any useful purpose. It simply articulates the presenter's self-consciousness—and the audience doesn't really give a damn.**

—"Gee, thanks a lot, Charlie, for putting me on the program right behind that fellow from L.A. I don't have any films or videotapes like he did—all I've got are some sheets of paper. But I'll try to make this as painless as possible for everybody."

This is the presenter being self-conscious about being badly prepared. The expectations of the audience aren't enhanced by this kind of talk, but it is essentially the presenter covering his own sense of inadequacy.

Here's another case of self-conscious palaver:

> "You know so much more about this subject than I
> do that I feel sort of silly getting up here and . . ."

The presenter is telling us that he (or she) is on shaky ground.

Phil Hoadley, a corporate banking executive of long experience, told me that a presenter who admits to knowing *less* than his audience is letting himself in for a *massive* dose of stress. It figures. The presenter has deliberately cast doubts on his own credibility.

And, finally, there is the type of palaver that is important to the presenter but causes needless concern for the audience:

"I think I feel a little indigestion coming on.
What do you say we take a break and I'll take a
bromo . . ."

This is telling the audience more than it really needs to know.
Now, the audience will begin to worry about the presenter and forget
about the presentation.
One final example:

"We have been on such a roller coaster here lately
that we're lucky to be here."

What roller coaster? Lucky? How come?
Palaver can provoke nervousness about the presenter. Yet presenters often feel compelled to reveal what's bothering *them* before they even begin to consider the needs of the audience.
Without further palaver, here are five suggestions for dealing with it:

1. If you feel that you must warm up your audience with a layer of palaver, get *one* person to do it—the first speaker. An audience doesn't have to be *re*warmed before every presentation. Once is enough (some meetings turn into *pure* palaver).
2. Be conscious of palaver. It's the filler, the guff, the platitudes, the "necessary words" that aren't really heard.
3. Resist the urge to chatter, self-consciously—to make excuses, or make amends for your inadequacies. It will simply draw attention to them.
4. Don't tell your audience what's bothering *you* if it really has nothing to do with *them*. Once you tell them that you're in trouble, they'll be troubled—distracted from the purpose of the meeting, and there goes your presentation!
5. Try an opening line for your presentation that goes right to the heart of your presentation. One of the most effective presentations in recent memory started with these three words: *"Information Reduces Risk."* Everything thereafter related to that singular thought.

Don't get me wrong. Palaver has its place, but it's not as harmless as most presenters think. And it consumes a lot of precious time.
If your presentation is running long, or seems slow—or any of those other complaints that are frequently made about meetings—the problem could be palaver.

34

The audience is much older—
or much younger—than you.
Either way,
the Age Gap can be trouble.

T hat kid can't be more than twenty-five years old—and he's up there telling *me* how to sell my cars. He's never run a dealership—never had to meet a payroll—never worked a used-car lot. What can he know? I'm supposed to let him spend my advertising budget? *He's just a greenhorn kid!"*

> *—An automobile dealer in Wichita watching his advertising agency present the spring advertising campaign.*

"Who is *that*? She's got to be fifty—maybe even fifty-five, and *she's telling us* about the trends in retailing. She reminds me of my Aunt Jane. I expected somebody like me—you know, *tuned in."*

> *—A magazine staffer listening to a market research consultant present lifestyle trends affecting the market place.*

The two presentations are occurring simultaneously—hundreds of miles apart.

The young business school graduate presents his agency's recommendations to a group of veteran automobile dealers in Wichita. Each dealer contributes a share of the advertising monies, so the dealer's involvement is intense, to say the least.

The market research consultant with twenty-five years of experience presents her company's findings to an editorial staff meeting in New York City. The average age in the conference room, *excluding the speaker,* is about thirty.

Both presenters are encountering the same problem.

They are talking to audiences who were expecting a presenter of a very different age—and, because of that age gap, the presenter's authority is being questioned.

It happens every day. It is not unique to any business, or any region of the country. And as more and more companies "restructure" their staffs, the middle levels are dropping away—being eliminated—leaving the bright, eager "young Turks" and the seasoned, traditionally oriented "mature executives." Often, they confront each other.

Resentment usually stays below the surface, simmering, yet coloring the discussion. And it creates a tension in audiences that can become a sort of self-induced guilt blanket. (Everybody *knows* the presenter's age isn't going to change just because it makes the audience cynical.)

What's to be done?

Here's a distillation of suggestions and insights from presenters who encounter the Age Gap problem almost every day:

1. *How you dress* is very important in situations where your age could work against you. If you're *older* than your audience, wear your least conservative outfit (that doesn't mean you have to come on looking like the latest creation from Paris—but it *does* suggest that you pick one of your livelier numbers from your current wardrobe). If you're *younger* than your audience, wear your *most* conservative outfit. This doesn't mean "somber," but it *does* suggest *seriousness*. You don't have to look like Daddy Warbucks, or a female version thereof, but it won't hurt to show them that you think this meeting is *extremely* important.

The point here is simple but sensitive: *Don't encourage negative stereotyping by what you wear.* Besides, for some of the more enlightened members of your audience, *attitude* is more important than *age*—and, for them, dress can be a mirror reflection of how you think about things.

2. *Consider the age of your language.* If you're *older* than your audience, go easy on the nostalgia and references to personal history. "Back when I was getting started in this business . . ." is an automatic tune-out for most audiences, particularly younger groups, no matter what the rest of that sentence turns out to be. Previous affiliations with now-defunct companies needn't be glorified. "I used to be national sales manager of the Hudson Motor Car Company," isn't going to impress many people.

George Burns can say, "You know, used to be—when me and Gracie were playing Peoria . . ." and the audience will howl. But listen carefully and you'll notice that he always relates his recollection to something that is happening *now*. The past is interesting only to the degree that it affects the future. Besides audiences *love* George Burns. Who else could puff on a monstrous cigar, sing off-key while shuffling through a small dance, and make us believe he's really a Casanova?

If you're *younger* than your audience, be careful of those phrases like "you guys" when addressing the whole group. Playful and affectionate though it may be, it can make a mixed audience of mature vintage *cringe*.

"You know" is another youthful phrase that irritates older ears. When used between every unfinished thought, "you know" becomes a ceaseless, shamelessly inarticulate reminder of the age differential. After a while, audiences may be tempted to say, "*No*, I don't know."

Don't let your language contribute to negative stereotyping. Listen for it when you hear yourself on tape—then do some self-editing on your next presentation.

3. *Keep in mind the one inexorable law of human nature that's working for you.* Whether your audience is quietly older or brashly younger than you are, here's the thing to put firmly in the front of your head when you get up to speak:

They are far more interested in themselves and their problems than they will ever be in how old *you* are.

Once you have accepted that snippet of psychology, your tactics become clear (and pretty easy):

■ Address their problems as *quickly* as possible and apply your *full* knowledge to the solutions. Do your homework. Don't let them think, for one moment, that you're giving them a "pat" presentation. "Generic presentations" simply won't work on audiences who think they're special. Show them that you have worked hard to help them, *really help them*, and the Age Gap will evaporate.

■ Don't patronize their age bracket. Don't give them the feeling that you're on the outside looking in. Just don't mention age *at all*. It's irrelevant. Once you get into answering their needs, it doesn't really matter how old you are, how tall you are, or whether you have had a slight stammer since childhood. What matters is how effectively *you* help them.

There are a few other points you may want to keep in mind, and no audience in the world will dispute either one of them:

■ Experience is a teacher that's hard to beat, and the only way to get it is to *live* a few years . . . usually quite a few. That's a nice little credential for presenters who have accumulated some hard-earned living time.

■ The future is usually reserved for the young. This may be unfair, but that seems to be the system. And the future holds a certain irresistible allure for almost everybody. That's not a bad break for youngish presenters who represent, for better or worse, *the future*.

Moral: Accept what you are, but don't give your audience any excuses to apply negative stereotyping. Actress and author Ruth Gordon used to ask this question: "How old would you be if you didn't know how old you are?" That's how old you want to be when you present yourself.

35

What audiences *know* (without being told).

Very few audiences have more than a modicum of knowledge about presentation technique. They have probably never heard of *group dynamics* (and couldn't care less). "Body language" is something that remains fairly fuzzy in their minds. And speech pathology is a course they *didn't* take, or even consider, when they went to school.

Yet, in some strange, mysterious way, audiences *know* more than presenters ever give them credit for. Audiences have a sixth sense that flashes sharp, clear signals to their brains—and the signals are invariably accurate. *Never underestimate the sensitivity of an audience.*

1. *Audiences know how you feel that day.* They'll read your energy level within the first ninety seconds. If you get up in the morning and don't know exactly how you feel, you'll find out pretty quick. Your audience will detect your feelings *and play them right back to you.* If you're grumpy, watch out! (*Personal Aside:* I call my eighty-six-year-old mother every day. The moment she picks up the phone and says, "hello," I can tell what kind of day she's had.)

2. *Audiences know if you don't like them.* Everything you do will seem slightly reluctant to them. Or confrontational. Almost every question becomes a problem. Voices get thin and edgy. A presentation where dislike simmers below the surface is *not* unlike the Titanic heading out to sea on a cold night.

3. *Audiences know when you've memorized your presentation.*

The act of memorizing instills the fear of forgetting.

Once the audience realizes that you're reciting lines you've memorized, (everything sounds like it was chipped out of granite), they'll start to worry if you're going to make it through to the end. Every pause will present the unsettling possibility that you have forgotten your lines. Moral: *don't memorize.* It's hard on you. It makes audiences uneasy.

4. *Audiences know when you're lying. They know when you're bluffing.* Eye contact crumbles. Voices grow thin. Your colleagues squirm. The moral: don't even *think* about lying. It alienates audiences like nothing else.

5. *Audiences know when you're giving them a sales pitch.* Something inside of them says, "This bird is trying to sell us a bill of goods." Contrary to all popular sales folklore, audiences don't like to be sold. They like to be entertained, helped, even *taught,* but I never heard an audience say, "Gee, I hope somebody tries to sell me something today."

6. *Audiences know when you've given up on yourself (they'll think*

you've given up on them). Recently, in a new business presentation for a $75 million national advertising account, the creative director—presenting a crucial part of the agency's effort to win the business—said "I've got this thing so screwed up I'll never get it straightened out." This was uttered as a sort of aside to himself, but it was loud enough for the audience to hear. Now, this kind of candor isn't a big confidence builder for an audience expecting to be dazzled. Can't blame an audience if they hunker down and expect the worst. This, of course, makes the presenter feel like he's been abandoned at sea. Moral: Even if the power goes off, the slide projector explodes, or the audience refuses to crack a smile at your funniest stories—plow ahead. Keep your poise. Keep your energy level up. Don't throw in the towel. Ovations are often awarded to those who survive.

36
"What's the burning issue here?"

Herb Zeltner is a marketing professional in New York City who takes part in a lot of important presentations with a lot of different companies.

He even counsels corporations on selecting suppliers via competitive presentations.

Herb has a question that can throw most meetings into a state of shock. It is so powerful that it must be used with caution:

"What's the burning issue here?"

Visualize this scene. You're sitting in the middle of a meeting that has been under way for close to an hour, and you quietly ask the question above.

What do you think would happen (pick one)?

- Stunned silence.
- Quick response.
- Confusion, some tittering.
- You would be asked to leave.

Many meetings don't entertain the possibility of a "burning issue." It just doesn't occur to them. Other meetings simply can't see "the burning issue" because of all the details that obstruct the view.

But you, as a presenter, should know that "burning issues" exist—and that someone in your audience may well ask a "burning issue" question. *Who* will it be? "Someone sophisticated and smart," says Herb Zeltner, "and, more than likely, the most senior person in the room." The question itself will be basic, but a bit "dangerous"— maybe controversial. Here are a few examples:

- The subject of the meeting may be redecoration of the lobby, but the "burning issue" may be "Do we even *need* a lobby?"
- The subject of the meeting may be recruiting new employees, but the burning issue may be "Why is turnover so high?"
- The subject of the meeting may be the weekly status review, but "the burning issue" may be "Why do we have so many meetings around here?"

The "burning issue" question jabs at the heart of it—probes at causes rather than effects.

For any meeting where you are presenting, ask yourself,

"What's the burning issue here?" and think it through. *It's an excellent exercise.* Maybe you include your thoughts in your presentation, maybe not. In any event, you'll be prepared.

P.S.: The next meeting you attend, consider asking Herb Zeltner's question. *"What's the burning issue here?"* If the meeting doesn't have one, maybe you can sneak out early.

37
The Man
in the Box

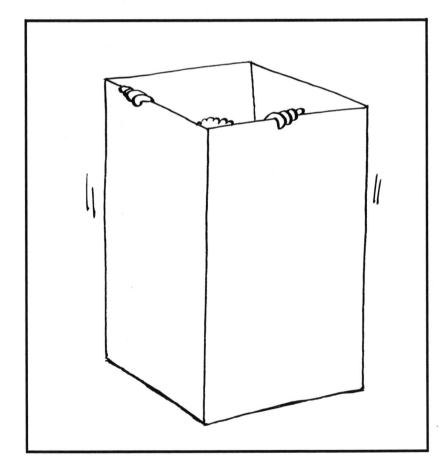

A young advertising man named Jim Wise gave one of the best presentations on making a presentation I have ever seen.

He's an art director, and when I saw him deliver his presentation, he was working for an agency in Atlanta, Georgia.

Here's how I remember it:

He moved quickly into his proposition: To really communicate with an audience, you've got to escape from the everyday routine of your own life and get inside the mindset of your audience.

Fair enough. His audience settled back to hear about it. But, like most outstanding presenters, Jim had a surprise for us.

He reached into his pants pocket and pulled out a roll of white tape. He kept on talking.

"You know, every one of us lives inside a box."

Suddenly he's on one knee. He begins to peel the tape off of the roll. With an art director's sense of style and proportion, he starts to form the outline of a box on the floor. He's using the tape, gently but firmly pressing it onto the carpet—*enclosing himself within the box.*

He talks as he works:

"Our boxes, for each of us, are the individual routines of our lives. We get up at the same time every day, brush our teeth with the same toothpaste, eat the same breakfast, read the same paper, take the same route to the same job, stare out of the same window—and probably say the same things to the same people. You know something? Your world becomes your box."

He stands up, still within his box—neatly formed on the floor. He looks down at the bars of white tape.

"You've got to get out of your box."

He steps out of his box and starts to walk around. He's looser now, the words seem to flow more easily. The dynamics inside the room change. The room itself seems bigger.

He proceeds to tell us how he looks at the world through another person's perspective.

"If I'm trying to understand a writer, maybe someone I'm working with, I'll sit down and try to *write* something—to see how it feels to fill up a page with words, or express a thought that I had only *pictured* in my mind before."

He then tells us about getting married and, on occasion, having an argument with his wife.

"Now I try to see it from her point of view (which isn't always easy) and when that doesn't work, I say to myself, 'How would Elvis Presley deal with this situation?'"

A funny thought, but the principle is serious.

Most of us operate, day after day, within the self-imposed confines of our own boxes. Presentations suffer from parochialism—from the ratings of "soapbox orators" who never bother to find out what their audiences are thinking.

Before you tell somebody else what to do, spend a little time looking out at that person's world.

Get inside, and look out.

It's not hard to do.

■ If you're going to make a presentation to an audience of stockbrokers, call your own broker and ask him or her if you can spend a few hours soaking up the atmosphere of a busy financial center. Listen to the calls come in. Where do the problems come from? Watch the stock prices change and see if you can pick up the patterns of the day. Note the language of Wall Street. See how it *feels* inside the pressure cooker of a broker's office.

■ If you're going to talk to a grocer's association, spend a morning in a supermarket—watching the manager, asking questions, sensing trouble spots.

Or, at the very least, get on the phone and talk to three or four store managers, "How's business? Where's the competition coming from? What's happening to produce prices? How do you see the future?" Tell them you're making an important presentation to the grocery industry. They'll talk to you.

Get out of your box and find out what's happening in all those other boxes, especially those boxes where your audience lives. Remember—they'll be evaluating you and your presentation from inside *their* boxes. Better know what it's like in there.

The young art director was finished with his presentation. He carefully removed the tape from the floor, but the symbolism of it stayed—indelibly imprinted where extraordinary presentations always leave their mark . . . on the memory of those lucky enough to have been there.

38
The audience needs a break—but when?

If you receive a message like this, sort of mashed and desperate looking, you've been presenting too long without giving your audience a break.

There are other "give me a break" signals and you should have no trouble detecting any of them.

Recently, I attended a one-hour and forty-five-minute talky, tedious drama *presented without a break*. About forty minutes into the tedium ("Aunt Dan and Lemon"), I started watching the audience, sketching the postures of bored people enduring life without a break:

Head down, right hand over eyes. Then, head down, left hand over eyes.

Examining glasses—squinting through lenses, as if they were at fault, responsible for what he sees, how he feels.

Head being held by hand, as if the head had lost consciousness.

Glasses off, arms crossed, right leg propped on back of chair, then the left leg gets the chair.

Hand rubbing something out of eye—trying to erase the scene, trying to stay awake.

One finger at temple . . . what does all this mean?

Head looking reso-
lutely away from
stage—refusing to
be involved. Hand
protecting brain
from damage.

Deep, heavy
sighs—"How much
more can I
endure?"

Pulling on ear,
resisting what he's
hearing.

Arms crossed, legs
crossed, head low
on chest. Trapped.
Besieged.

Knuckles rapping
quietly on the chair.

It's amazing how tolerant and polite audiences are. They can survive a lot of pain, but in an audience that needs a break, you can always detect the ceaseless body movement, the nervous fidgeting, the shifting of weight, the scuffing of shoes, the restless discomfort of needing to be "released"—to take a break.

When things get too insufferable, audiences often resort to more direct means.

■ Someone will shout out, "How about a break?" Others will chime in, reluctant to be the first complainer, but more than willing to join the chorus.

■ One by one, they get up and leave. They don't say anything. They just leave. Everybody knows where they're going.

When the audience is doing everything from writing "desperation notes" to trooping, one-by-one, out of the meeting room, you—as the presenter—have a duty to perform.

Call a break. Let the poor devils go.

But you know it and they know it: *you have waited too long.* It's always best to anticipate the needs of an audience rather than to respond to them once they have become urgent.

There is a rule of good sense to be observed in most cases: Give your audience a break every half-hour. A break doesn't have to be more than five minutes, but it should be stricly adhered to:

> *SUGGESTION:* When you call the break and give your audience a specific time at which to return, appoint someone in the audience to be responsible for getting everybody back on time. This does some interesting things. It makes that person feel important. It creates a little good-natured fun. And it removes the "herding" job from your shoulders and allows you to do other things (more about that in a minute).

The idea of a break every half-hour has many precedents. Most television shows don't last over thirty minutes. Many sporting events are broken into halves—a National Basketball Association half, for example, has twenty-four minutes of actual playing time. Most plays and musicals are broken up into two or three acts (except for the tortuous *Aunt Dan and Lemon*), and you seldom find a show that runs much over two hours.

If people get uncomfortable sitting for long stretches of time at Broadway hit shows and professional sporting events, what does that tell you about your presentation?

No offense intended—but you owe those people a break. It's just good manners. "Oh, oh"—says the presenter—"I'm not so sure I want to do that. I have been allotted a certain amount of time and I've got an enormous amount of material to cover." Or, "If I call a break, I'm liable to lose my audience." Or, "We're usually running so far behind schedule, there's no time for breaks."

> *Here's the point:* the minute you start to worry about yourself—how much *you've* got to cover, how late *you* already are, whatever—thereby ignoring the condition of your audience, you're headed for deep trouble. Audiences invariably put *their* needs ahead of *your* needs. It's not even close.

"Breaks" can be very useful for *you* as well as nice little rewards for your audience.

"Breaks" give you a chance to take a reading on how you're doing. If your audience has been unresponsive, ask a few people for their off-the-record comments. Maybe something's happening you didn't even know about (they're worried about a management change, they're concerned about a possible client loss. Who knows? But, after you're informed, you'll be better able to cope, and the more you know about your audience, the better).

Taking a break will give you a chance to do something about any nettlesome problems you've noticed. The room is too hot. The room is too cold. The ventillation sounds like a thrashing machine. Lights are flickering. You can, at least, *ask* if anything can be done. (It's always better to get it fixed during the break, not during your presentation. Maintenance people on stepladders are tough competition.)

Well, here they come—your audience trooping back from the "break." Maybe you've made a few editing changes based on the comments you've heard. Maybe the room is functioning better. Maybe one or two of your colleagues have made some insightful suggestions.

One thing's for sure: *Your audience looks better* (maybe they got good news when they made those phone calls). Most important, they're grateful to you and ready to give you their undivided attention. You've got a better chance now. And that encouraging realization should be good news for *you*.

39

How to eliminate audiences and start reading faces.

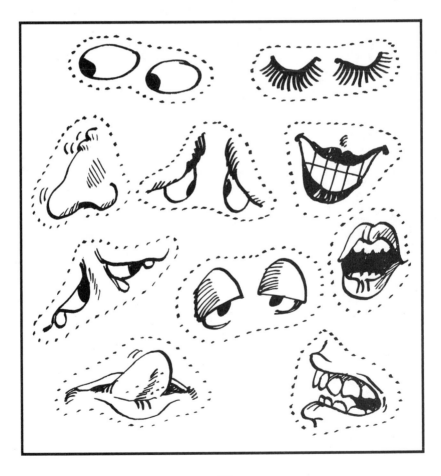

Professional golfers don't really see the hazards that terrify run-of-the-mill golfers.

A huge lake in front of the green? Forget it! Let's concentrate on the ball going in the hole.

That's the way it is with professional presenters, too. They don't really see the audiences when they're presenting. They concentrate on individuals. They strive to connect one-to-one, one person at a time.

This eliminates the audience hazard, reduces nervousness, and vastly improves communication.

There's something else about professional presenters that you should know. They look at individual faces a bit differently than ordinary people do. They see eyes, ears, mouths, foreheads, and other aspects of facial geography in terms of what they suggest or symbolize to the presenter.

You've heard of body language.

Let's examine facial language—and see what you, the presenter, can learn from it.

FACIAL LANGUAGE

Furrowed forehead means problems with acceptance.

Same for eyebrows.

Any placement of the hand over face is a signal of apprehension, hesitation, suspended judgment.

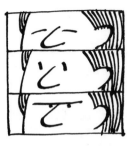

Final verdict registers in eyes first.

Eyes are the best indicators of interest. May range from "riveted" to asleep. This man is glazed.

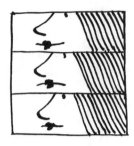

Also a good indicator of interest. Ends of mouth up: agreement; down: disagreement; straight: judgment pending.

"When is that presenter gonna start talking about *me*?"

Type A—Intense, eager, concerned, fretful (typical new business prospect).

Type B—seeking entertainment, diversion (typical luncheon club member).

Your audience: daydreams easily.

Retains nonverbal impressions. Forgets 90 percent of what he hears.

Is extremely time-conscious (except Type B).

40

Body Language:
It can sound an alarm
without making a sound.

Body Language: A knotty case that *could happen to you.*

You may never meet this person. But it's possible that he or she may show up at some kind of interactive meeting where you are the presenter—and that person will be important to the outcome of your meeting.

Let's say the person is a man—in his mid-forties, well dressed, an executive—sitting on the aisle in the third-row center. He may never utter a word. In fact, it's possible that you didn't even notice him until your presentation was almost over.

Then, you become extremely conscious of him. He has arranged himself into a body language that is disturbing. It sends out signals. And the signals are like warning flags, waving silently in the wind.

This one person's case of body language is well worth examination, since he's giving off some signals which are easily recognized—and can usually be fixed. Let's see what this fellow looks like.

Who is this man and why is he avoiding you?

He's probably a nice person—sitting there in one of those funny wraparound desks you find in old classrooms. But his body language, for all of its indolence, is sending out signals that you, as the presenter, must be able to read.

This man has checked out of your presentation. He's there, but he's gone. Not only has he mentally excused himself, he is physically retreating. The body language couldn't be clearer.

Everything about him is leaning away from you. Even his head is averted. His eyes are open, but they aren't making contact. His body is slumped, sort of draped backward over the desk. He has wrapped himself up in his own limbs. One arm protects the chest, grasping the other arm that is thrust into a pocket—out of action (you'll notice his notepad has been abandoned—another distressing signal). His legs are crossed, defensively. He's given his feet over to the presentation and withdrawn his brains. What else? Glasses are off—apparently he doesn't need them any more, but his wristwatch is evident, exposed just under his drooping head. Resignation, that's what it is. He's sitting there, all self-constrained, waiting for the presentation to be over.

How on earth could this man be dangerous to you? Because other members of the audience are aware of his attitude, and it could be catching. Or maybe he's the boss of the group and they think he's giving them his opinion of the presentation. He's creating a cloud, a negative presence, and the dynamics in the room could be turning against you. One person's body language can do it, particularly if that one person carries a certain influence. *What should you do?*

How to cure a bad case of body language.

In treating a bad case of body language (like the man on the aisle in the third-row center), you've got to bite the bullet and assume that *you're* the problem. Or at least a sizable *part* of it. Maybe he disagrees with your point of view. Maybe he's heard it all before. Maybe he feels left out. Maybe you never really addressed *his* problem. Maybe he thinks you stole his thunder. Whatever the reason, fair or unfair, his body language and facial language are telling you exactly how he feels at that precise moment.

It is time for some rather intense sublety. He won't appreciate it if you suddenly zero in on him. Don't patronize him. But you can begin to work on eye contact with him, reducing the distance, showing your concern. Once you make any kind of connection, get any kind of response, you can ask him if you've covered everything he needed to know. Give him time. It will take him a few seconds to rouse himself. Let your concern show. If he remains unresponsive, don't give up on him (*never* give up on an audience). Back off, move on, circulate. Don't let one person pull your energy level down. But don't hesitate to return to him. You're not angry. You're not pushing. You're not confrontational. You're *concerned*—genuinely interested in him. (Maybe, just maybe, you even *like* him.) Ask him what his experience would suggest. Stay with the eyes (it's your strongest avenue of access), inviting him to contribute. Once he changes his body language, straightening up, shifting toward you, you'll feel a difference in the entire room. The cloud is lifting. The meeting is moving forward again.

There's an old saying from somewhere, "People lie—body language never does." Infallibility may be pushing things a bit—but it certainly won't hurt to keep your eye on the guy in the third-row center.

41

"If you don't give
me a list . . ."
(Audiences just love "do" lists.)

It was break-time. I had been presenting to a group of bankers in New England—and the first half-hour of my presentation was over. There was another hour to go.

People were lining up at the coffee table, picking up doughnuts and bowties, then moving into little clusters of conversation.

A young woman of about thirty was nipping into a chocolate doughnut and trying not to spill the cup of coffee she had just filled. She was standing by herself, and I decided to do a little research.

"Give me your honest opinion," I said. "How am I doing so far?"

She smiled pleasantly, munched on her doughnut, and thought about it. I could tell from her nice, open expression that she was going to tell me exactly what she thought.

"Well, good," she replied. "Maybe good *plus*."

"Any suggestions?"

"I'm finding it a little hard to take notes," she said. "I think people like to be given *lists* of things, don't you?"

"Yes, I suppose." I had never really thought about it.

"Oh, yes. If you don't give me a list, how can I write my report? If I can't write my report, how can I prove I was here?"

She sipped her coffee. Everything was under control.

"An audience like this—most of us anyway—are expected to write a report to our superiors. You know, just to prove that we were here. Without notes, it's hard. We need lists."

She was so sure of it, so logical, so *right*. Tell people you have six things for them to do and they will instinctively pick up their pencils and start writing. It must be a carryover from high school. Or some kind of deep-rooted association of lists with matters of substance. A list, no matter what it says, communicates nonverbally—"Here's something you'd better remember."

Suddenly, after this young banker had explained everything to me, it all became quite clear. If you don't give your audience an itemized list or two—they may subconsciously think you're not giving them anything worth writing down. It becomes an excuse not to listen, an opportunity to daydream (which most audiences love to do anyway).

There are additional rewards in this wisdom about "lists." If you have ever been told that your presentations lack content, put in a list or two. You'll find that in making the list you'll compress your information and it will indeed become more substantive.

Mention the *number* of items on your list. It's magic. Note-taking will accelerate like crazy. You'll *feel* the activity in the room—bodies moving forward in their chairs, pages of notepads being flipped, papers being rustled in the search for pencils and pens. The place comes *alive*.

Help them as much as you can. Orchestrate the ritual. Maybe you write the items on a blackboard or a flipchart (this gives your audience extra time to make their notes as you're guiding them through your list). Or maybe you create a "build"—which is nothing more than a series of slides, each slide adding a new item to your list.

Caution: Don't hand out lists. This gets people involved in reading instead of being led by you. It's often difficult to get their attention back.

After learning the importance of lists to people seeking knowledge (and having to report to their bosses), I vowed that if I ever wrote a book—I would pepper it with lists of all kinds. You'll find one in almost every chapter.

42

Nerve Endings.
(Insensitivity can overpower
any subject.)

There's a pearl of presentation wisdom that says audiences react to "personal affronts" more quickly than individuals do. It's true.

An individual may shrug off an insensitive remark, thinking that it was inadvertent and, besides, it was no big deal. ("I was the only one to hear it, and maybe I took it wrong.")

When that same remark slips into a formalized presentation that is heard by a *crowd*—the reaction cuts through the room and becomes an offense against the organization, or the locality. It cannot be pardoned or ignored. *Everybody heard it.*

The presenter might just as well pack up and catch the next plane out of town. The message has been doomed by the presenter's violation of a highly sensitive nerve ending.

How many of these seemingly trivial but utterly destructive errors have you heard (or maybe even committed yourself)?

■ *A sarcastic reference to the city you're visiting.* Let's say you've been invited to Buffalo to address a local business group. It's snowing. You've had a terrible time getting to Buffalo. Planes were delayed. It was murder. You get up to speak, cast a sorrowful glance at the falling snow, shake your head, and say, "Well, here we are in beautiful, downtown Buffalo." The audience smiles and cringes simultaneously. You move into your message. *The audience isn't hearing it.* They *live* in Buffalo, have *homes* in Buffalo, do *business* in Buffalo. They were probably even *born* in Buffalo. They *love* Buffalo—and they are sick of people taking pokes at Buffalo.

Presentation Ethic #1: Don't knock the town you're in. People are extremely sensitive about where they live. They *like* it. Wherever you go, to make a presentation or simply to conduct business, it's a great place. You're *delighted* to be there. And it shows because *you mean it.*

■ *An unflattering reference to a specific age group.* Picture this (it happened): A marketing director gets up to report to her management on future plans. She speaks of broadening the sales program to include consumers from fifty-five to sixty-five years old, noting—in passing—that these more mature individuals may dilute the "youthful image" of the product—but "older people" have vastly increased buying power.

Sitting there in the audience is a vice president of the corporation *who just turned fifty-five.* He prides himself on his youthful waistline, attitude, and sex life. He hates anything that makes him feel "old."

This presentation has just alienated him from the presenter and shattered any chances of the program being approved.

Presentation Ethic #2: Do not make editorial references to age. If you must mention specific ages, beware of stereotypes. People over sixty are not necessarily *"senior citizens."* People over forty are not necessarily *"middle-aged."* These terms can put you in a deep freeze, and no presentation—no matter how brilliant—can pull you out. Here's a little something to keep in mind: *You never know how old people are.*

■ *An unappreciated greeting to someone in the audience who is having a horrible year.* This happens at sales conferences all the time. The sales manager rises to greet his audience. The room is teeming with salespeople. They are brimming with optimism and bright expectations. The sales manager's gaze falls on Charlie (everybody knows good, old Charlie). The manager's words of encouragement boom out to every corner of the room:

"We're particularly glad to have Charlie with us for this conference. It's been a tough year out there in Charlie's territory and we're all rooting for Charlie to get a lot of good ideas during this conference so he can go home and do the kind of job we all know he can do."

Charlie, meanwhile, is withering. He wants to crawl under the carpet. Then, just to finalize the awkwardness, the sales manager shouts, *"Right, Charlie?"* Everybody looks at Charlie. Charlie smiles a smile that only an executioner could love.

Presentation Ethic #3: Don't draw attention to poor performance no matter how worthy your intentions. One person's morale is never lifted by words of encouragement that identify the individual as a loser.

■ *The misplaced use of "contemporary colloquialisms."* Our language has been liberalized. There's the F-word, and the A-word, and the S-word, and words that defy definition. They just sound ugly. Most of the words are adjectives (especially the F-word). Their meanings may be hazy, but they communicate a certain defiance of polite society. Recently, I attended a new business presentation involving a prospective client for a marketing organization. The client was a huge service organization. In the old days, it would have been called a public utility.

The prospect had sent seventeen representatives to the presentation.

After the first break, an account executive rose to address the elusive issue of "corporate culture." As his enthusiasm grew, his language became a bubbling brew of "contemporary colloquialisms." There were all the conventional four-letter words, plus some five-letter varieties you don't hear very often (genitals get a lot of attention in today's vocabulary of swearwords). There was one man in the audience, about sixty I'd say, whose body actually convulsed a little every time he heard one of those words. I watched him carefully. It was like somebody grazed him every few minutes with an electric prod. His body language attempted to cover these jolts he was receiving (he'd cross his legs, cover his face, slouch in his chair—nothing worked).

He just physically *recoiled* from the language he was hearing. He, of course, was the senior representative of the prospect's contingent.

Later, when the business had been awarded elsewhere, I asked the account executive why he used so much salty language.

"Oh, they love it," he said. "They talk just like that all the time."

Yeah, I thought. All of them *except one*.

Presentation Ethic #4: Watch your language. What may be colorful and contemporary to you may be offensive to certain members of your audience, and they may be the very ones you want to influence. If you don't hear it on network television (please notice I didn't say "cable"), don't use it in your presentation. As far as I know, the use of blue (or purple) language has never helped a single presentation.

■ *A seemingly casual touch, on the arm, the neck, the waist, wherever, to show a sense of cooperation and mutual involvement.* When the presenter *touches* a member of the audience, red lights flash through the heads of all others in the room. "What's going on there?" When the presenter touches a member of the opposite sex, clanging bells join the flashing lights. A touch, innocent though it may be, can carry implications that far transcend your message. *Besides, most people don't like to be touched.* It can be patronizing, or demeaning. (I used to have a boss who would wrap his arm around my shoulder and clasp me to his chest. He was about 6'5" and it made me feel like Charlie McCarthy.)

Professional Ethic #5: Outside of shaking hands, don't *touch* your audience. Don't invade their "private zone"—which is the area within twelve inches of the face. Yes, there are television game-show hosts who *kiss* everybody. That's different (I find it equally nauseous, but it *is* different). Game-show hosts are regarded as "members of the family" and family members *do* kiss occasionally. Presenters like you and me aren't entitled to deliberate physical contact. That's taking unfair advantage of our role as leader, teacher, presenter. We can be touching emotionally, intellectually—but, please, do not touch.

■ *A defensiveness that incites you to criticize the criticizer.* You've made your presentation and you ease into the question/answer section of the meeting. Part of your recommendation is under fire—and it's a part that you tailored, very carefully, to the specifications that your audience gave you. You really took great pains to make it fit what they told you were their requirements. Yet they're *questioning* it now. One person in particular won't leave it alone. You've had enough. You blurt it out, "Look, it just so happens that you're the one who asked for that feature. I didn't want it. You're the one who *made* us do it."

Suddenly, the criticizer is being criticized. Suddenly, the presenter is the prosecutor—"not my fault," he implies, "*your* fault!" The audience has been put on the defensive. The presenter has destroyed his own authority by shifting responsibility away from himself. It's a no-win situation. It's also curtains for the presenter's proposition.

Presentation Ethic #6: Don't turn the tables on your audience. They can criticize *you*. But if you criticize *them* for criticizing *you*, you've lost them. You can reason with them, but you can't ridicule them. It may be tempting at times, but what you'll gain in gratification—you'll lose in votes.

■ *An irritating tendency to forget the names of key people in your audience.* People don't like to be called "Harry" if their name is "Tom." Names are very personal. They were given to us by our mothers and fathers. If you ask a person what she thinks of a particular subject, and you call her "Martha" when her name is "Marlene," she's going to get the impression you don't really *care* what she thinks about the subject. And if you call a person "Malcolm" when his first name is really "Forbes" (as I did for almost an hour), the rest of the class is going to start to giggle. Your authority flies right out the window.

Presentation Ethic #7: Get a list of the names and titles of the people who will be in your meeting. Say the names out loud at least ten times each so that you connect the right first name with the proper last name. If it's a conference room, have nameplates identifying seat locations (this will eliminate all the confusion that usually starts with, "You sit there—no, I think over here would be better").

If it's theater-type seating, have nameplates that stick on and peel off easily (not the ones that *pin on* and make holes in your clothes). Of course, the best solution is to *know* everybody's name and greet them instantly—by name. This requires names *and pictures* well before the presentation date. The logistical requirements of knowing names *and* faces before a first meeting can be demanding (especially if it's a large group), but if you've got names, pictures, and a reasonably good memory—you'll be the hit of the day. People notice it when you use their names. They may not say anything, but they're impressed. They remember you—and, if you're lucky, they remember *your* name.

■ *Not knowing what to say about smoking.* In a meeting room, where you have ten or twenty people involved in a presentation, what happens when somebody takes out a pack of cigarettes and casually lights up? These days, *everybody* notices. Some people don't mind. Some people sort of resent it but don't say anything. And a few people *fume*. If those who resent it and the few who fume happen to be customers or prospective clients, or other guests of importance and influence—you've got a real ticklish situation. Here's the rule:

Presentation Ethic #8: As a presenter, you *never* smoke. If you're the world's most compulsive smoker, you steadfastly refrain from smoking at your own presentation. If your team of presenters is hosting an audience of important guests, nobody on the team smokes during a presentation. If one of the guests lights up, you act like you don't see it. But here's the point that may be tough for some smokers to accept: *even if a guest—an "outsider"—starts puffing away, the presentation team doesn't smoke.* The reason is simple: the audience isn't going to *like* you any better because you smoke (unless you're soliciting a congregation from the American Tobacco Institute), but somebody may simply "tune out" if you or any of your colleagues fill the room with smoke. Violate a nonsmoker's "space" and the presentation is over. You have committed a "personal affront" to the sensitivities of some people.

■

None of these eight sensitivities *sound* like presentation-busters. But all of them *are*. They rattle people *emotionally*. They stick in the craw. They make you so memorable (in a negative way) that your subject becomes *instantly* forgettable. Beware of the exposed nerve ending. It may not seem dangerous, *but* it can be lethal.

43

Test your mettle
as a presenter.

W̲hat would you do?

1. You are seven minutes into your presentation to an executive review committee. Things appear to be going well. Suddenly the chairman of the committe gets up and heads toward the back of the room. He (or she) goes to the coffee urn and pours a cup of coffee, then starts browsing through the Danish pastries. He isn't paying the slightest attention to your presentation and everybody in the room is conscious that "the boss" isn't listening. *What would you do?*

Recommended Action: The continuity of your presentation has been broken. If "the boss" isn't with you, nobody else will be with you either. Might as well tell the chairman he's got a great idea and invite everybody to have a cup of coffee and be back in five minutes.

2. You're in the midst of a presentation of ten people. It's 11:00 A.M. The door opens and it's the head waiter (your meeting is in one of the large hotels in town). The waiter announces that he is there to take luncheon orders. He whips out his order pad and looks expectant. *What would you do?*

Recommended Action: If you're near the end of your presentation, tell the waiter to return in five minutes (or whatever amount of time you'll need. *Be specific* about the time). If he gives you an argument, don't get angry. Be prepared to call a break. You'll find that most audiences are concerned about food. It's hard to compete with it, particularly around mealtime.

3. It's 2:10, and your meeting was scheduled to start at 2:00. Everybody is there *except* the highest ranking officer. People are starting to get restless. It's your meeting, you're the presenter. *What would you do?*

Recommended Action: Turn to the *next* highest ranking officer and ask that person if you should start or wait. Keep your voice low, but loud enough so that everybody in the room knows what's happening. And knowing who's responsible for the decision is especially important if you're presenting to a client, customer, or prospect. By quietly consulting the next-in-command, the decision is "theirs," and nobody will be mad at *you*—particularly when the highest ranking officer comes thundering in twelve minutes later and says, *"Who started this meeting?"*

4. You're sailing along, nearing the end of your presentation. A

questioner raises a point. You try to answer. Somebody else jumps in, cutting you off. Before you know it, a verbal battle breaks out between the questioner and the interrupter. They're really going at it, back and forth, and you're left on the sidelines. *What would you do?*

Recommended Action: Let them thrash for a few minutes. Some audiences *need* to argue amongst themselves (it makes them feel better). Once the battle starts to subside, step back in and take control. Be prepared to articulate the areas of agreement and move briskly back on track. Humor is often effective when a presentation veers wildly out of control. Ed Rosenstein, an exceptional market research analyst and presenter, would drop to his knees, clasp his hands together in mock supplication, and shout above the din, "Please, God, where did I lose control?" When an argument is broken by laughter, it's generally a good time to steer the group right back to your subject.

5. You're the first presenter after a big, elaborate lunch. Your audience is full of food—and wine. A person sitting up front is on the verge of being drunk. He's certainly tipsy. He won't shut up. He keeps interrupting you, asking what is essentially the same question *over and over. What would you do?*

Recommended Action: Answer the question. Stay calm. Try to rephrase your answer each time you respond. Don't laugh at him. Don't be sarcastic. Keep answering the question as best you can. Eventually, one of the man's colleagues will tap him on the shoulder and whisper, "Let's go get a cup of coffee." If you are a guest in somebody else's organization, *let them take care of their own.* This is terribly important. The moment *you* start to discipline the mischief-makers, you'll lose the sympathy (and admiration) of your audience and *you'll* become the culprit.

6. You're making your presentation, moving along smoothly, when you realize that you are looking into a *sea of glazed eyeballs.* Your audience has drifted away from you and you don't have the faintest notion *why. What would you do?*

Recommended Action: If you have lost your audience, and you don't know why, call a break. Ask your colleagues for their observations and suggestions. Obviously, there has been a breakdown in interest. Do the obvious: *change.* Change the presentation area—give your audience a different set to look at. Change the subject—move along to your next topic. Change the presenter. Maybe just a new face and a fresh voice will bring the audience to life. The worst thing to do is continue in the same style, on the same subject. Your audience will turn to stone. Most presenters can sense it when an audience has lapsed into daydreaming. At this point, you've got little to lose—*change!*

7. You're on a roll. All systems are performing perfectly. You're showing some 16mm film and the film snaps. The projector makes that awful sound of loose film slapping against metal. Your audio/visual technician gets busy, struggling to splice the broken film. He is flustered—and the situation looks bleak. It could be a long wait. The audience looks at you, wondering how you're going to handle it. *What would you do?*

Recommended Action: In this case, it's very important to know what *not* to do. Here are some "*don't* dos":

■ *Don't* get mad.

■ *Don't* just stand there.

■ *Don't* start rattling off jokes that have nothing to do with the situation.

Here are five things you *can* do:

■ *Declare* a five-minute break and see how long it will take to get things going again.

■ *Go on* to something else that doesn't require broken-down equipment. Hope that repairs can be made in the meantime.

■ *Open up the meeting* for questions or discussion of the material covered to that point. A trifle risky, but probably okay if the vibes have been good. If they haven't, maybe you can clear the air.

■ *Tell a brief story* that relates to the situation. If you're not good at telling stories, try the following.

■ *Say something like this:* "Have you ever had a day when everything you tried went bad? When, no matter how hard you worked, things got *worse?* I have days like that all the time. Do *you?* Well, our audio/visual engineer is having one of those awful days. Let's just hang in there with him (or her) for another five minutes and show that we understand." This plaintive plea puts the audience in the shoes of the person in the control room or wherever the unlucky A/V engineer happens to be, and probably keeps things reasonably peaceful for about five minutes. The last time I heard a speaker use those words (or something like them), the audience not only settled down, *it applauded.*

8. You're presenting to a group of executives known for their toughness. You're moving into your proposition, and the audience is looking good. Then, with no advance warning, the chief executive officer says—in a brash, gruff voice—"I've read your material, and I

think you're full of crap." A hush settles over the room, and the CEO looks you dead in the eye, waiting to hear what you've got to say. *What would you do?*

Recommended Action: You don't do what you feel like doing. You conquer the urge to grab your easels and slide drums and stalk out the door. You look *him* dead in the eye and say, "Okay, fair enough. Tell me where you had trouble and let me see if I can help you." You meet *rudeness* with *helpfulness.* You diffuse the hostility—keep yourself under control—and concentrate on the issues. If you're patient and helpful—and he's abrasive—eventually, someone will say, "let's get on with it." Chances are, the CEO is just testing you anyway. So regard it as a little corporate game-playing and not a challenge to your character or professionalism. Keep cool. It'll pass—and you will survive the situation with honor intact.

44

"Hold that temper!"

This is a cardinal law of presentation:

Never, ever lose your temper. There are tons of reasons, but here are the main ones:

1. *You are probably being tested.* People who lose their tempers are not in great demand. If you get angry, under a heavy barrage of questions or a storm of unsolicited comments, you are not likely to be invited back. The person in the audience who's taunting you is probably testing your flame-out level.

2. *Presenters who lose their tempers are regarded as "out of control."* Self-control is mandatory these days—in all aspects of human conduct. I don't care whether you're a minister or a Wall Street tycoon, you'd better be able to control yourself. A wildly careening temper marks you as *uncontrollable* trouble. Therefore, you are socially and professionally *untouchable*.

■

There aren't a whole lot of temper-taming techniques (which is probably just as well). Take these two precautions and you should be all right:

■ When you feel your temper heating up, tell yourself you're being tested. Repeat, please, after me, *"This is only a test. This is only a test."* Think of it as a fire drill. Bells are ringing, but you are going calmly to your station. Tempers react most violently when they sense that something really *important* is being suddenly violated. "This is only a test" will help you put things back in proportion.

■ Write down, word for word, the two most infuriating questions you're likely to hear. Put the *questions and your best answers* on an audio tape and play them back until you can listen to them without getting upset. This will do two things: it will take the shock factor out of the hottest questions imaginable (all others therefore move down the temperature scale) and it will help you answer questions rationally that would otherwise have you on the brink of rage.

Anger casts a pall over a presentation that is impossible to dispel. "Cool it before it heats up, or banish it before it starts."

45

"Hey—
you've drawn
a *crowd!*"

Most presentations are to groups—from ten to twenty people, gathered around a table or loosely assembled, theater-style.

Let's assume something good about you.

Let's assume that you have gotten so effective at presenting to groups that you receive an invitation to present to a crowd.

So, what's a *crowd*? Fair question.

I have always maintained that a group was any gathering of *less* than fifty people—and a crowd was anything *over* fifty.

But let's take no chances on arbitrary definitions. Let's be definite about you and what you've been asked to do.

You've been invited to address a gathering of five hundred people. That, no matter how you look at it, is a crowd.

What are you going to do differently, now that we've mutliplied your usual audience by a resounding *fifty-fold*, more or less?

First, let's admit that there *are* differences—in general atmosphere, presentation skills required, and certain communications limitations that the sheer mass of a crowd imposes.

A bit earlier in this book, there was a chapter titled, "The audience is a car, idling. You are the accelerator." That was a chapter about generating intensity and a sense of urgency in a relatively small group (twelve) of people. The audience was symbolized as a car ready to roll.

A crowd of five hundred people is more like an aircraft carrier. It's harder to get it going, harder to turn it around, and it's always got all kinds of activity happening on deck—planes landing, planes taking off, planes getting hauled and hoisted about. Being the speaker before a crowd of five hundred is not unlike being the captain of an aircraft carrier.

If you've attracted a crowd of five hundred, you're going to be up on a platform somewhere, not unlike the bridge of a ship. You're elevated, separated from your audience. That's *one* difference from presenting to a group.

You're also going to be farther from most members of your audience than would be the case with a group of ten or twelve people. You're not going to be able to involve yourself as easily—either physically or philosophically. Distance does that.

Since you're up above and farther away from your audience, you're going to be limited in several technical respects. Eye contact is going to be difficult, and probably impossible with people sitting in the back. That's an important consideration and requires some adjustments in technique (more about that in a minute).

Also, participation by members of the audience may have to be minimized or sacrificed. People are not as eager to participate *individually* in front of a crowd. (In fact, they often like the anonymity that a crowd provides.)

Still another consideration: crowds—like carriers—have all kinds of activities going on most of the time. People coming in, going out, shuffling, and hustling about. Think of any convention you've attended lately. Constant hubbub.

So, a crowd is different from a group in significant ways.

Now, let's get back up to the bridge where we can calmly administer the resolutions to these difficulties.

Presenting to a *group* is a one-by-one process. You speak to the people individually. Presenting to a *crowd* can't be done on a one-by-one basis. There are just too many people. But a crowd can be regarded as a single entity, a single unit, like an aircraft carrier. It's *yours*. Yours to understand. Yours to control. The crowd is not five hundred people. It's *one* entity—and you got it!

If you'll accept that concept, the solutions to our previous difficulties will appear immediately:

■ *Your mission is to keep an eye on the crowd,* maintain contact—not to establish individual relationships. That means you demonstrate your awareness of everybody by letting your eyes rove into all four corners of your audience as well as the heart of it.

■ *You move,* physically, to increase your exposure to the entire audience—as well as to demonstrate your sensitivity to all of them. Also, movement by you generates alertness in them.

■ *You project your voice and yourself more forcefully,* just because you've got more space to fill and it's going to take more energy to get things moving your way.

■ *You don't get upset if you notice a few people sneaking out.* They will probably be replaced by a few people who will slip in the side door. Crowds are restless creatures.

■ *You don't try to operate all of the A/V aids by yourself.* Captains don't go down and fire up the engine room. Make sure you've got back-up systems if your slides jam or your video segment fails to show. Nothing inspires confidence and authority in a speaker like a great audio/visual technician.

■ *You remember your crowd psychology.* People react much differently in crowds than they do on their own. They join the flow. This means that once you feel a surge of approval from a crowd, it's likely to gather momentum. By the same token, if a crowd drifts away from you, it's hard to turn it around. Crowds are like aircraft carriers.

■ *There are Type A crowds and Type B crowds.* Type A crowds are intense, eager to learn, critical. Example: The Young President's Organization. A Type B crowd is there to be entertained, or for the social satisfactions.

Type B crowds are more likely to be interested in the meal than the speaker. Example: The Rotary Club. Do your audience analysis. Know which crowd you're talking to. Lighten up for the Type Bs. Knuckle down for the Type As.

■ *Keep your presentation within an hour*—shorter if possible. The reason: you're working without the benefit of truly focused eye contact. That limits your ability to hold attention for long periods of time. This is where electronic audio/visual techniques find their most useful niche. They can enlarge the image of the speaker (often, to horrendous effect) or they can create attention *around* the speaker that doesn't rely on close eye contact.

One final point about *you* and crowds.

Crowds are flattering. Not everybody can draw a crowd. *You did.* So, step up and take command. *The crowd is yours.*

46

Your best chance
to work a miracle.

It's the night before your big presentation.

You have just run through your final rehearsal for a group of randomly selected colleagues.

The response has been polite. The tone has been considerate. The comments have followed this general pattern:

> "Well, I'm sure it will be just fine when you actually do it tomorrow."

This usually means, with the politeness ironed out, "It didn't do much for me. Maybe the *real* audience will get something out of it."

There's also the comment that comes from a candid "Stanley Kubrick" at the end of a dress rehearsal for a crucial presentation.

> "Look, it's one hell of an effort—but it's not going to win. It's not going to get us past the competition. It's got a lot of good information in it, but it simply isn't connecting. It's not strong enough—as a presentation—to carry the day."

You sense that Stanley is right.

You sense that everybody is right.

You also realize that it's midnight and your presentation is scheduled for ten o'clock tomorrow morning.

You've got to work a miracle. Overnight. *How do you do it?*

First, let us dispense with the "don'ts."

1. *Don't junk everything you've got and start over.* This is always disastrous. You'll drive yourself crazy. Your head will be a jumble. It's too late for new game plans.
2. *Don't stay up the rest of the night and feel guilty.* Don't sit there and tinker with your presentation. Don't worry it to death.
3. *Don't call up and cancel.* Cancellation is another word for capitulation.

So much for the "don'ts." It's time for some heartfelt "dos."

1. *Do start thinking positively.* Tell yourself you not only *can* carry the day, you *will.* The reason: You're not going to trash your work, you're just going to turn it a bit.
2. *Put a simple idea in your head.* Here's the simple idea:

"I'm going to put the words 'you' and 'your' into my presentation as many times as I possibly can."

All of a sudden, things are looking up. You've got a positive attitude. You've got a simple, straightforward strategy. You can sleep.

Next morning, the strategy becomes blatant, overt. You're going to inject some blatant, overt references to your audience's self-interest.

"Now, let's look at it from *your* perspective . . ."

"Here's what that means to *you* . . ."

"What's in this example for *you?*"

"Here are some things that *you* can do . . ."

"How can *you* profit from this?"

Want a role model for this strategy? Try Louis Rukeyser, the amiable moderator of *Wall Street Week*. Listen to him:

"Now, what should our viewers do? Would you advise them to buy or sell?"

"Can you give our viewers a few stocks that you think will do well in the months ahead?"

"What exactly does that mean to the individual investors in our audience?"

Rukeyser is always bringing it back to the audience, always pinning it down, always making it more useful for the viewer.

That's *your* strategy, too. You're simply turning your message toward the needs of your audience.

"Now, let's relate that to *you* and *your* situation."

The more "yous" and "yours" you add, the better. You'll see it in the response of your audience.

PART SIX

How to deal with questions

A NUGGET FOR YOUR NEXT PRESENTATION: *"Consider questions as compliments"*

"Questioning" has gotten a bad name. Maybe it started in those old movies where the cruel captain bellowed at the lovable first mate, "Are you *questioning* me, sir? How *dare* you!"

Or maybe it started in the courtroom when the stern judge said severely, "I'm not going to allow that line of questioning."

Wherever it began, questioning causes queasy stomachs in many presenters. Here's a way to think about it that can help you take the fear out of it:

NUGGET: Questioning is an expression of genuine interest in your presentation. There are no hostile questions, only defensive answers. Welcome every question. Consider it a compliment—and be thankful.

47

What "no questions" really means.

You have just concluded a resounding summation of your main point, hammered home your themeline one last time, and thanked everybody for being so gracious.

You're finished.

Applause ripples around the room.

You stand back and wait for the first question.

Nothing.

You survey the audience expectantly, waiting for the first hand to go up, the first questioner to start a spritely dialogue.

Quiet. *There are no questions.*

You say what everybody says in this awkward situation, "Well, I guess that means I *answered* all your questions." The room titters. You sit down or slither out a side door.

What does "no questions" *really* mean?

There are a variety of interesting possibilities, but "no questions" rarely means the audience is totally satisfied. It generally means that there's something wrong somewhere. What are the possibilities?

■ *You have gone at it too long.* Your audience is exhausted. You've overwhelmed them. They haven't got the energy to ask a question. They're eager to move along to the next meeting, catch a train, find the nearest bar, or watch a ball game. They don't want to hear any more about your subject—and they'd probably strangle the first person who said anything that even *sounded* like a question.

■ *You stepped on a sensitivity somewhere along the way.* You didn't mean to. You just said something that alienated the whole crowd—and they *tuned out* at that point.

It doesn't take much to "freeze" an audience. Just say something chauvinistic to the League of Women Voters. Or crack a lame joke about the local football team. Hit a raw nerve and your audience will abandon your subject, and dispense with questions. (See Chapter 42 on "Nerve Endings.")

■ *Your audience has already made up its mind* to cast its vote elsewhere. This happens. You were invited to present—but the outcome was a forgone conclusion. The winner was already in the clubhouse. When this happens, you'll probably hear about it later. Don't let it throw you. Competitive presentations aren't *always* what they seem.

■ *You never quite reached them.* Some audiences listen attentively but the presenter never really connects with their daily lives. The subject remains abstract, distant, theoretical. An eloquent presentation about "the indomitable sea lion" as a symbol of inspiration is going to be lost on a bunch of factory workers who have just been fired. They'll listen. They'll watch. They may even applaud. But the speech won't elicit many questions.

■ *They got muddled in the middle of your presentation* and couldn't muster the energy, or the interest, to stay with you until the end. By the time you had finished, they didn't really know what you were talking about. Bewildered audiences seldom ask questions. They don't like to admit they didn't understand it, and they won't struggle to make sense out of it. They just sit there. Quietly.

■

Some audiences simply don't ask many questions. Oriental audiences regard questions as a form of criticism, so you won't get a lot of questions at the Nippon Club. But, for most audiences, the asking of questions means that you have whipped up enough interest to create a desire for more information.

"No questions" usually means what it means in a courtroom. "You're excused. You can leave now. We're through with you."

That's not what an effective presenter wants to hear. But now at least you know some good, hard questions to ask about your next presentation:

■ Is it too long? Too heavy with detail? Have I told them *so much* that I have obscured my main point? Have I saturated their brains with information they don't really need? Have I *suffocated* them?

■ Am I stepping on any sensitivities that could override my subject and turn off my audience? Have I said something that cuts too close to the bone?

■ Is my subject of no earthly interest to these people? Have I selected a subject that interests *me* but is a yawner for them?

■ If it's a competitive presentation, had the winner been selected before you even had a chance to tell your story? (Nothing you can do about this. Just keep your poise and give it your best shot.)

■ Am I talking above their level of interest? Is my message too theoretical, too fancy? Does it simply fail to talk their language?

■ Is my message absolutely clear? Do I have any gaping disconnects in my logic? Will my audience drop through the holes?

Don't be afraid to ask tough questions of your presentation to make it more provocative to your audience. If *you* are your toughest questioner, your presentation will generate plenty of response.

48

Questions that
top executives like to ask—
and some suggestions
that may save the day.

If you find yourself in a presentation to a group of top executives, particularly chief executive officers and/or presidents, there are certain possibilities, or likelihoods, that you'll want to keep in mind:

■ Top executives frequently ask questions that they have asked before and, in fact, *know the answers to.* So, why do they ask? Answer: they want to know if *you* know. Evaluation of employees, consultants, and advisers goes on all the time. It is a continual, almost automatic, activity for most top executives—and it can save a lot of time in the evaluation process if the executive knows the answer to the test question. This doesn't mean it's an easy question. It's probably a question of considerable importance to the executive, one that he or she asks regularly of different people to get a deeper understanding of it.

Suggestion: Do a bit of detective work. Ask some of the CEO's aides if there is any particular question, or series of questions, that comes up frequently these days. What's the subject of greatest concern? You will undoubtedly get a question related to that concern—even if the question has been expressed before.

■ Top executives often ask questions that are (A) of transcending scope, or (B) of almost impossible precision.

    A. "Can you give me an idea of where your recommendation fits into our five-year corporate strategy?"

    B. "Do you have a month-by-month cost comparison of this operation with our plant in Atlanta? What's the pay-out plan on each installation?"

Executives like to say, "What are the *implications* of this?" They also like to say, "What are the *key figures* here?" You've got to be ready for both ends of the spectrum.

■ Or, the question may fly off into some totally unpredicted but astonishingly pertinent area. "Where did you people ever get the idea that the consumer really gives a damn who makes her grocery sacks?" The best executives think through the minds of their customers. It's not a bad channel for the presenter either.

■ Top executives can also be caught thinking their way through a thickly complex issue, and articulating it in the form of a thickly complex question. Example: "If we were to make an analysis of our corporation in terms of its corporate identity before and after the merger, how much of our total communications budget should we allot to clear up the confusion that I strongly suspect exists?"

Now that's tough. A hypothetical situation requiring some highly problematical assumptions.

There are a good handful of ways to deal with convoluted questions of that kind:

1. Ask to have the question repeated so that you can be sure you understand it. (As the question is repeated, you'll probably find that it gets shorter and clearer. But it may also change in emphasis if not in meaning. Your mission here is to gently help the executive think his or her way through the troubling issue and then provide your best answer.)
2. *You* repeat the question as you understood it (that will probably prompt the executive to clarify *your* clarification and you will have more time to consider your answer).
3. You request a few minutes to think about it. The question may just go away.
4. If you really *do* understand the question, relate it to a similar situation in your experience. This will provide an answer to the question, but won't lock you into any specific action until you can obtain more facts.

If there's a CEO in your audience—and that person is the boss of everybody else—the sooner that CEO asks a question, the better it is for you. It will send a signal to the others that will clear the air—and get *everybody* participating.

49

The "short form" list
for answering questions.

Let's say you have just made a stimulating, substantive presentation to a group of anywhere from ten to fifty people.

More than likely, you'll get some questions.

Whether you get questions or not, *you should always be ready for them*—because Q&A, as it's called, is where presentations enter "the real world." The mood changes. The audience shifts from passive to active and begins to close the gap, if there is one, between *your* proposition and *their* immediate situation.

You should have a pretty clear idea of who's going to ask what questions and what you're going to say in response. That's not always precisely predictable, but if you've done your audience analysis—and you know your subject from *their* point of view—you're going to find that answering questions is not only satisfying, it's sort of fun. It's nice to be asked for your wisdom.

There are "long forms" for dealing with questions raised by cost-cutting managements at budget review sessions, and there are "short forms" for shorter presentations dealing with less complex subjects.

Since it may be some time before you are called upon to justify your department's cost allocation to the budget review committee, let's look at the "short form" which will help you at almost any presentation where questions are likely to arise.

The "Short Form" Process for Q&A

1. *Anticipate the questions you are likely to get. Write them down on yellow tablets,* leaving about six ruled lines or empty spaces between questions. You'll find the questions will come easily to mind if you know your audience. People ask questions about the issues of greatest concern to *them*—their positions in the organization, the problems affecting them *that day.* Sales managers ask about sales promotions. Corporate communications directors ask about images. Personnel managers ask recruitment methods. And *everybody* asks about costs. If you've done your homework, you'll be able to anticipate at least *70 percent* of the questions you actually get. The President of the United States does even better—*85 percent,* according to recent reports. Of course he's got a staff of experts trying to figure out what's bothering each one of the White House correspondents on any given day, especially days when press conferences are held.

2. Once you've got all of the likely questions written down on your yellow tablet, run your eyes over them. *If you've got more than twenty questions, chances are high that your presentation is a little loose*

and needs to be tightened up. Maybe you should answer some of those anticipated questions within the body of your presentation. NOTE: The process of anticipating questions is a superb exercise for testing the strength of your presentation. Questions which elicit more detail are *good.* Questions which point up gaps and holes are *bad* (better answer those in the main part of your presentation).

3. Once you've got your anticipated questions down to a manageable size (under twenty), *go back and answer each one—as best you can—out loud, into a microcassette recorder.* It's no big deal. No pressure. You're not making a speech. You're just giving the recorder your best thoughts on the questions you're likely to hear.

4. *Now, let's listen to what you said.* Play your answers back to yourself. Impressed? This is where your yellow tablet gets into the act again. In a different color from the questions, make notes under each question that will strengthen each answer. Pertinent facts. Vivid phrases. Maybe even simple, little sketches to help you remember the fresh points you want to add to your original answers.

5. Using your yellow tablet of questions, your notes to yourself (written after hearing your first cassette), *answer the questions one more time on a fresh tape.* When you listen to the second cassette, you'll notice a stronger content to the answers *and* greater assurance in your voice. If you're happy with the second tape, use it as a way to keep engraving those strengthened answers into your memory. Maybe you listen to it when you're driving to the site of your presentation—or while you're eating breakfast that morning. Pretty soon you feel as confident about your Q&A session as you do about the more formalized part of your presentation.

6. *What do you do about the 30 percent of the questions that you probably won't anticipate?* If you don't know the answer, say so. Write the question down and tell the questioner you'll have an answer for him or her in a specific length of time (twenty-four hours always has a nice ring to it). By writing the question in plain view of your audience, you demonstrate to the questioner that you *too* think the question is important. If you don't have a detailed answer for the unanticipated question, there's nothing wrong with a short, crisp answer. Most busy people prefer brevity. A "yes" or "no" is often more responsive than a reply that drones on forever.

7. *Write, at the very bottom of your yellow tablet, a nice, clear summary of your proposition—including "the next step."*
Example:

> "Research shows this company is associated with
> old, established products that are no longer growing.

> I propose that we investigate the acquisition of a
> small company in the health-care field. The next
> step is a thorough, discrete analysis of the three com-
> panies I have suggested."

It's just one paragraph; no more than three sentences. But it's the *heart* of your presentation. Keep relating your answers to it. Use it to keep questions from wandering too far afield. Make sure *the core* keeps coming through. In Q&A, you're always working your way toward that succinctly worded summary statement.

A Far-out Idea That Works

Include a few far-out, "extremist," questions on your list. And have some good, serious answers ready. That way you won't be shocked into silence when a few sizzling firecrackers land at your feet:

> "Is this all you have to show us? We like to see *lots* of
> alternatives."

> "Those are big city ideas. We do things our own way
> around here. Have you checked with the merchants
> down on Main Street?"

> "Your plan sounds good. Now show us how you cut
> the cost to us by 25 percent."

The secret to answering questions is being ready—anticipating and preparing. The seven steps in this "short form" will help you do that. There's one more thing that will help you. It's attitudinal rather than technical. Think of it this way: *Every question you get is an immediate expression of interest in your presentation.* There's no way in the world that can be bad.

50

How to handle questions that are really suggestions.

S*napshot:* It is the delicatessen convention on the boardwalk in Atlantic City. Various companies representing delicatessen products are having their sales meetings in the committee rooms of the flamboyant Trump Plaza.

Low-salt salami is up for discussion in one of the meeting rooms. It's a new product and salami salesmen in the room are excited about it. The presenter of the new item is a young manager, in his late twenties, and he's using a big chart to point out the specifications of the product.

Suddenly, one of the more mature salesmen (he looks like the Willy Loman of the salami trade) has a question. He holds his hand high and waves it around.

"Hey, why don't we list the ingredients on the side of the package and put the calories on there, too?"

"Interesting, Charlie, but we've already printed up an inventory of labels in these new, iridescent colors and we didn't consider labeling calories."

"But I watch the young people in the stores these days and they really read those labels. They want to know about calories and chemicals—they're really into it. Especially on a new item like this."

"Well, I'm going to see how these labels work first, Charlie, then maybe we'll get into calorie-labeling or something of the kind."

" . . . just thought I'd ask."

That was that. I watched Charlie sag into his seat, hands covering the lower half of his face as if to stop himself from saying anything else.

He listened as the next product was introduced (new baked ham loaf), then slipped out of the room.

I figured Charlie wouldn't be asking many more questions. He had the look of a man who might be visiting the casino, or the bar.

■

Granted, the manager handled it badly. But maybe we can learn something from what happened:

■ Charlie wasn't asking a question. He was offering an *idea.* Questions are frequently used to express ideas. They often get adopted more easily. *But the presenter has to know an idea when he or she hears one.* A question that has a concept in it is likely to be an idea.

■ If it really is a good idea, tell the group it will be reviewed with the package designer in terms of feasibility.

■ Tell Charlie you'll get back to him *by a specific date* with the decision on his idea—and thank him in front of the group.

This little docu-drama at the delicatessen convention isn't going to win a Pulitzer Prize but it does make a practical point.

Many questioners aren't really seeking answers. They're seeking *approval.*

Sensitive presenters can detect the difference. There's much at stake. Charlie's important. And his idea just might be a world-beater.

PART SEVEN

Learning from
those who cast a spell
and stay with us forever.

A NUGGET FOR YOUR NEXT PRESENTATION:
"Be a bit of Springsteen"

Bruce Springsteen is one of America's master present-ers. He presents ideas, attitudes, himself. In a recent article on Springsteen, *Newsweek* described the singer's presentation style as "a complete commitment to the immediacy of the moment." Precious few of life's experiences allow *you* to approach the kind of commitment that Springsteen makes in every performance. Presenting is one of those rare experiences.

NUGGET: Put a bit of Springsteen in your next presentation.

51

The most electrifying
presentation I have
ever seen.

I shall never forget it, no matter how old or how jaded I become. It lasted only five minutes, but it changed my life.

He was a young man, no more than twenty-five or twenty-six. He stood up before a small group of his coworkers, neatly dressed, but slender almost to the point of fragility.

I can see him now—maybe six feet away from me, tall and thin—talking quietly, but with almost tangible intensity.

"I have what is politely called a health problem," he said. "I have had it since I was a child. I started losing weight. One week I lost twenty pounds. The next week I lost fifteen. The doctor said I would never gain those pounds back again.

"The doctor gave me one of these." He walked over to a nearby table and carefully removed a hypodermic syringe from its case. The barrel was empty. He reached into a sack and took out a blue vial. He punched the needle into the top of the vial and drew the plunger upward. It was then that I noticed his hands were shaking. I thought he was nervous, trembling from the experience of making a presentation before his peers.

He returned to the center of the room. He held the hypodermic instrument up for all to see. "The reason I am shaking so badly is that I haven't had my insulin injection yet today. I usually take it when I first wake up—about seven o'clock—and now it is ten. I'm late. But I wanted to show you exactly what I have to do."

He bent his right arm at the elbow and made a fist. I felt frightened for him. He positioned the needle halfway up his arm, then pushed it into his vein just above the elbow. Silence.

"There," he said quietly. "It's really quite simple. Quite easy. Look." He extended his right arm and it was shaking slightly, but not nearly as uncontrollably as before. "I guess I am a little nervous," he said.

He went on to tell us how diabetes had changed his life. "I probably look at life a bit differently than you do," he said. "I see each new day as a gift, a bonus—and this needle is my friend."

His quiet, intense voice never faltered. "If you have diabetes, or have ever wondered about having it—I'd like to talk to you, to tell you what it's done for me. I don't think you'll fear it anymore."

The young man sat down. The audience was silent, stunned. Suddenly, my personal problems didn't seem nearly as serious. Then, there were murmurs of agreement, understanding. There was a feeling that we had shared something almost therapeutic. I felt *different*.

The "picture" of that young man with the syringe poised above his arm is forever imprinted on my mind and his quiet affirmation of life is an integral part of it.

In a presentation, things that are personally important to you always come across with great impact.

You don't need notes or a script if you're talking about life and death matters. Especially when they're your own and they apply to *everybody.*

52

"Tell me about *you*."
The dynamics of Donahue.

Watch Phil Donahue "work" an audience for sixty minutes and you will see an absolute master of crowd control. Some people might call it group dynamics, which is the term to use if you're a behavioral scientist. Donahue is *not* a behavioral scientist—at least not formally. He's a sort of synthesizer. He presents controversy, but manages his audience so adroitly that explosions seldom occur. He's an inquiring father/confessor in a labyrinth of volatile possibilities. Donahue has his own style which might best be described as conversational earnestness—but he's never too earnest to smile when a guest or member of his audience gives him a verbal poke in the ribs.

When Donahue had two life-term inmates from the Rahway, New Jersey, state prison on his show (via satellite), he professed surprise that the inmates would favor the death penalty. The more talkative of the inmates said, "Why, Mr. Donahue, I'm sure you've been surprised a lot of times by what people say on your show."

Donahue laughed, probably thinking of all the people who *have* surprised him by some wacky comment—but you also got the feeling that Donahue would say something unexpected but perfectly appropriate if *he* were sitting behind bars down in Rahway with absolutely nothing to lose.

That's the thing about Donahue. He seems able to identify with *everybody*—whether it's a life-termer in Rahway or a housewife from suburban Chicago. He gets inside of people's heads and ventilates their feelings, but he does it in such a way that you feel he's really learning a lot. His curiosity seems boundless. He swings off of one person's opinion and into another, knowing full well that the feminist from Highland Park isn't going to agree with the criminologist from the big city. He hovers over both sides with the same fair-handed style, "Let him make his point, Mrs. Jones . . ." His objectivity may be a bit suspect, but his manners are impeccable. He may tilt to one side of an argument or another, but he is never overbearing.

Though he is always well briefed by his staff, he gives the impression that he is really warming up to his subject. Gradually, artfully, his point of view emerges. Often, it is a melding of the best arguments from each side of the issue. It may become more clear-cut, more dogmatic, but it never loses the sound of moderation. When he sees heads nodding, he shares the credit with his audience. "Isn't that really what we're talking about here today?" he asks. Heads nod more vigorously.

When he breaks into somebody's long-winded argument, he'll say, "Excuse me, I want to get back to your point in just a minute—but first we've got to take a break." When he returns, he may come back to the windy person in the audience, or he may not, depending on the way he wants the program to flow. He's like a judge on the move, swinging from defense to prosecution—treating each side decently—not patronizing anybody. All the while he is seeking opinions, thrusting the microphone like it's some prized award for having a coherent or colorful point of view.

Donahue is a remarkable blend of intensity and good humor. He is everybody's oldest brother. He's the one who takes charge in an argument, giving both sides their due—or he could be the thatch-topped, youngish-looking uncle who obviously loves everybody and doesn't want anybody to go away mad.

When a person disagrees with Donahue, Phil may look a little quizzical, shaking his head in good-natured disbelief—then turn to one of his guests and ask, "Does that make any sense to you, Mr. Rothenberg?" Generally, Mr. Rothenberg agrees with Mr. Donahue. In a courtroom, this might be called "leading the witness," but on "The Donahue Show," it's sort of "All in the Family."

When Donahue talks, he may stumble a little—but not in such a way that you ever feel sorry for him. It's likable stumbling. His intentions are good. Never the bully, he has the same quality that James Stewart has. He's just too darn likable to do anything wrong. And he's really interested in each and every one of us. When he says, "Tell me about *you*,"—doggone it—he really wants to know.

Watching Donahue—Picking Up Pointers

1. If you're presenting a subject to a group, keep the dialogue conversational. Don't let intense feelings burst into flames. Keep the subject moving around the room.
2. Clarify carefully—credit merit. Respect your resisters. Be a good distiller. "Isn't *this* what we're really trying to say here . . . ?"
3. Make an honest effort to get everybody involved. Reach out to them.
4. Protect the soft-spoken and inarticulate. Don't let the big talkers clobber the people who can't get their thoughts out. Direct traffic.
5. Have a good time. But demonstrate that you're really involved in this subject—and that the truth is going to serve, perhaps even *save*, them all.

53

Why can't presenters be more like dancers? Lessons from *A Chorus Line*

Most people think of Michael Bennett's *A Chorus Line* as a song-and-dance show; a smash hit musical. And indeed it was. Not only did it win a Pulitzer Prize, among other prizes, but it has become the longest-running musical in the history of the theater.

But maybe, without taking anything away from its brilliance as a musical, *A Chorus Line* can be gainfully studied as something else.

In a very literal sense, it is a show about *presentations*, about different people presenting themselves to each other and to their boss (the choreographer/director played by Michael Douglas in the film).

A *Chorus Line* is a show about being able to express yourself, as accurately as possible, by stepping forward and making a spontaneous presentation.

That, in fact, is exactly what the final contenders for the permanent jobs in *A Chorus Line* are asked to do.

Remember the scene? The preliminary auditions are finally over (three thousand dancers actually auditioned for the film). The rejected dancers have been sent away with a cool, "thank you very much."

Now, the seventeen finalists remain—waiting for further instructions. The director calls the dancers with a phrase that is marvelously open to interpretation. He puts them "on the line" and asks them to step forward, one by one, and present themselves ("real name, stage name, where were you born . . . what makes you tick").

"If you can't handle it, now's the time to leave," he says. The challenge is real. The boss is serious.

The dancers seem uneasy, reluctant, nervous. But, *they need this job*—and, one by one, they try to explain what they are all about.

They are quite different—and that is one of the recurring themes of Michael Bennett's original story:

Within the apparent sameness of the dancers of the chorus line, each person is different, singular, unique.

Some of the presenters can't find the words to describe themselves and can only do it comfortably through dancing.

Some of the presenters ramble, resorting to cliches, searching for endings. ("I can't just talk. Please, I'm too nervous." "Let's be honest . . . you know what I mean.")

And some of the presenters remember times that are terribly

self-revealing. ("Hello, twelve"—wherein "Mark" tells us how it is to be twelve and suddenly aware of sex. "Nothing"—wherein "Morales" recalls that when her instructor in acting school tells her to *feel* the roles she must play, she feels "nothing." And even when he dies, she felt "nothing.")

Each presentation tells a story, projects an attitude, defines a character. We understand, at the end, what makes them different—and the same.

If you watch and listen to *A Chorus Line* as a presenter, you learn a lot. (I saw the play twice in New York and the film twice in Chicago.)

■ *"Keep it sharp. Make it strong."* Those are shouts of instruction from the dance director, but they apply to every kind of presentation. There is no sloppiness in an effective presentation. No half-hearted gestures. No waffling or hedging. Everything has a *crispness* to it. A confident, clearly discernible rhythm.

The worst thing that can happen to a presentation is for it to lose its focus, its sense of direction. To turn gray.

Dancers know where they're going. They're beautifully *prepared*. In this sense, as well as many others, dancers and dancing provide a prototype for all types of presentation.

■ *Use your mirror as a judge.* In *A Chorus Line*, the dancers are surrounded by mirrors. They practice in front of "dance mirrors" without the slightest suggestion of self-consciousness. They know what kind of image they're projecting because they have seen their reflections so many times before. The mirror judges the presentation.

The dancer corrects, perfects. Do all types of presenters do this? Do business executives study themselves in mirrors? Well, if they're buying a new suit or sports outfit, they do. They scrutinize every detail of cut and color. But if they're presenting *themselves* to a mirror, they may regard the whole idea as too *self* conscious. Strange, isn't it? If you can evaluate a coat in a mirror, you should give *yourself* the same opportunity.

■ *A clear sense of self-identity is essential.* There is a moment in *A Chorus Line* which is absolutely riveting. A young woman (Cassie), the exlover of the director/choreographer, walks downstage and says it's her turn to present herself. She demands her turn. He resists. She *insists.* "I'm a dancer," she says, "let me dance for you," and she starts to dance. Her image repeats itself, flashing in and through countless mirrors, *a singular sensation* multiplied over and over.

Presenters, generally, should follow Cassie's lead. Identify your strongest strength and project it as earnestly as you really feel about it.

What is your strongest strength as a presenter?

■ *Give us some snapshots to remember you by.* The dancers in *A Chorus Line* seem to be well aware of the pictures they create for your eyes. Watch Sheila, the veteran of countless chorus lines. She moves up to the line, moves her left leg across the right, slides her left hand up to her hip, and forms a snapshot in our minds. It registers instantly as grace, sex, and monumental confidence. Head erect, eyes alight, teasing smile—*click!* We've got a picture of Sheila that characterizes her, distinguishes her. She is one among seventeen, but different.

Most presenters give you pictures that have yet to develop—Polaroids that remain white. Don't be reluctant to project yourself in visual terms. Demonstrate something. Dramatize something. Show us something.

■ *Don't let the fear of rejection stop you from being sensational.* In Richard Attenborough's book about the filming of *A Chorus Line,* the actress who plays Sheila (her name is Vicki Frederick) tells what it's like to present yourself. "You just have to go in and be judged over and over again. Lay yourself on the line."

Which is really what *A Chorus Line* is all about, which is really what presentation is all about—you step forward and present yourself. "This is how I turned out," is what you're saying, whether you're a dancer, a politician, a teacher, an executive, a salesperson—and your audience is poised to render its judgment. Fair enough—upward and onward. You'll improve—every time. Your next presentation will be your best. As a matter of fact, you could be a *singular sensation.*

PART EIGHT

Afterwards—Some things
to think about
that will make your
next presentation
even better.

My daughter is a social worker in Evanston, Illinois, and her caseload is demanding and draining. She tries to help people with their problems—and sometimes she's successful and sometimes she isn't. But she's seldom down in the dumps. I asked her how she maintains her professional poise, how she handles the disappointments that can seem like disasters. Her answer struck me with such force that I had the words framed. It's a marvelous quote for "after the presentation," when you may feel sort of dubious about your efforts.

NUGGET: "Compared to eternity, it's really small potatoes."

54

The art of
compassionate criticism

Criticizing the presentation of a close friend or business associate can be like hopping through a bed of hot coals. As Dr. Seymour Hamilton, a professor in Calgary, Canada, and a former presentation coach of political candidates, told me: "You want to tell them how bad they really are, to *help* them—but you don't dare. It's too sensitive."

Presentation is such an intricate melding of personality and message that it is often difficult, if not impossible, to make a helpful criticism of the message without deflating the personality. And a candid comment about the *delivery* of the message can cast a cloud over the message itself. ("If I can't work up any enthusiasm for this crazy idea, maybe I shouldn't be the one presenting it.") It's tricky business, the critiquing of presentations, but here's a simple, little process that works. It works not only on the criticism of presentations but on almost any kind of creative effort:

1. *Find something good to say about it.* There must be something. The top football coaches don't haul a player out of the game and berate him for what he's doing *wrong*. They start out by telling him what he's doing *right*. Presentation is fueled by self-confidence. You have to keep that confidence alive, refueling it, before you can stand a chance of fixing the problems.

2. *Characterize the presentation before you criticize the presenter.* Give the presenter your impression of the *total* presentation before you get personal about the flaws of technique and delivery. Was it an "entertaining" presentation? Was it an "analytical" presentation? An "eminently reasonable" presentation? How would you characterize the presentation in a word or two? It doesn't have to be favorable. It could have been a "discursive" presentation. Or, maybe even a "disturbing" presentation. Whatever its effect on you, describe it.

This will give the presenter a general "environment" in which to place your more specific comments later on.

3. *Keep the focus of your critique clearly on the future.* "We're talking about your *next* presentation, and how we can help you make it the best one of your life." Presentation style is hard to change. It becomes ingrained, a part of behavior, as habit forming as a golf swing that has stroked some very good hits. By critiquing the presentation *now*, you aren't knocking what has worked in the past, you are simply offering suggestions for the future. Keep the emphasis of your critique where it does the most good—on "the next presentation."

4. *Be specific.* A criticism that "it just didn't seem very interesting" isn't going to help the presenter. You'll probably get a look that says, "You're a big help . . . how about telling me what I can *do* about it?" So, you tell him or her. "Use some examples from your own experience." "Make your gestures broader—think of yourself as a traffic cop." "How about starting with a question that addresses the problem head-on?"

Most presenters don't really need to be told they're deadly dull—it doesn't do much for the ego. But they'd probably appreciate it if you told them exactly how to get an audience off their duffs and actively engaged in a presentation.

5. *"Make it useful for everybody."* It's a lot easier to accept criticism if you feel that you're not the only person on earth who's got those same problems. Maybe, just maybe, what you've learned will help somebody else. The great coaches say, "Look, let's learn from each other." And it works beautifully.

Example: A presenter gets up and seems hesitant, tentative. Why? She's embarrassed about being short. "Only five feet tall," she says in a shy voice. Somebody else says, "I feel the same way because I'm so darned tall." Out of this exchange comes a realization that can be useful to everybody. *Being different is only a problem when you make the audience feel uncomfortable.* If you present with self-assurance and authority, nobody is going to fret about the fact that you're five feet tall—or whatever distinguishes you from other people. They'll admire you for what you are. That's a discovery of universal value that came out of one presenter's experience.

55

"Here's looking at you, kid!" —on viewing your *first* videotape

*L*et's *look at the tapes.*

Looking at videotapes has become a part of the game in collegiate and professional athletics.

If a team in the National Basketball Association, for example, has been trounced in a big playoff game, the scrutinizing of the tapes may start immediately following the game and continue into the early morning hours—then resume again after breakfast with coaches and players viewing and reviewing crucial actions.

The New York Times quoted Detroit Pistons coach Chuck Daly, following his team's 1987 playoff loss to the Boston Celtics.

> "There is only one way to stay on top of it; when you watch it on films. Only then can the players and coaches see what went wrong. There are no make-believes with the films, and sometimes it takes a couple of viewings before it sinks in."

Aspiring presenters should listen closely to Coach Daly (who, like many coaches, tends to use tapes and "films" interchangeably when, in fact, tapes are magnetic tape, and film is film).

Videotapes of you, presenting, can be invaluable as you prepare for your next presentation.

What you'll see isn't you *live* (videotapes tend to flatten people out), but it's you as you *were* when the cameras were rolling, and it's probably the most realistic motion picture of yourself that you'll ever see. As Coach Daly says, "There are no make-believes with the films."

You may discover that you're ignoring half of your audience—or seeking inspiration in the ceiling. You may find that you're smiling self-consciously—or scowling heavily when you weren't even worried. You may want to speed up your voice, or slow it down, or *calm* it down.

Or, you may realize that all of those little tics and twitches that you thought were so bothersome *aren't even noticeable!*

You'll know what to fix and what to leave alone. You'll have a picture of yourself that you can modify as you see fit.

It's an exciting prospect, isn't it? If you've never seen yourself on tape before, you'll have—for the first time in your life—a perception *of you* that is based on your reality, not somebody else's.

So, you've done it. You've made a tape. You've videotaped a rehearsal or the actual presentation. (The equipment can be rented with a phone call, and rates for suitable cameras are modest—$75 or $85 for the day, plus tapes. You can even rent a cameraman, if you want, but the minimum goes up to around $175 for the day plus an hourly rate of $18.)

You slip the tape (according to your unit's directions) into your videotape player (VCR) and snap on your receiver. The screen lights up and, in a few seconds, *there you are!*

You are presenting to yourself, seeing and hearing yourself as your audience sees and hears you. You are the audience for you, the presenter.

Your first videotape can be a landmark experience in your life, moving testimony that you *exist*, and—in all honesty—it can also be a trifle unsettling.

Here are some tips to ease the trauma and chart the course:

—*Be an audience of one at the first viewing.* Just you, alone. That way, you're less likely to be defensive. You, looking at you for the first time, can create considerable self-consciousness, especially if someone else is watching you watch yourself.

Just sit there (it's best to be sitting down for your first viewing) and observe yourself *out of sheer curiosity.* (You'll be tempted to say, "Is that really me?" It is.) So, relax—lean back—and get used to the sensation of seeing yourself from *outside* rather than *inside*.

—*For the second viewing, become your boss,* or whoever your most critical audience may be. Try a little role playing. Look and listen to that presenter on the screen as if he or she were working for you. Would you be impressed with your good judgment in hiring that person up there? If you were your boss, how would you characterize the speaker's greatest strength, and most troubling weakness? What would you tell that presenter if you were the boss and wanted to pass along a few words of compassionate criticism?

—*Look at your videotape with the sound turned all the way down.* This will show you, silently, how you are communicating *nonverbally*. With the sound off, you'll become aware of the "chemistry" you're projecting. Are you animated or staid? Do you smile or frown? How's your poise? Are you comfortable? This, of course, leads into all kinds of other questions you can try on yourself, "Do I trust that person? Do I like that person? Would I want to see that person again tomorrow?" Looking at the *nonverbal you* can provide a dramatic and revealing portrait of how you are perceived as a presenter.

—Now, push that sound back up and look away from the screen. What does your voice alone tell you *nonverbally?* Would you want that voice to be the captain on your next long-distance flight? Does that voice *know* anything? Does that voice *believe* what it is saying? It's absolutely amazing what your voice can tell you just by its tone, texture, and general attitude. Some presenters discover, with a little help from the tapes, that their *words* don't really match up with their nonverbal communicators. Example: the words can be urgent—the delivery can be off-hand, uncaring. Guess which message the audience takes away?

—For the fifth viewing, invite a colleague to watch your tape with you. Turn on the tape (you'll be an expert by this time), and position yourself in the darkened room so that you can watch your audience out of the corner of your eye. Watch your visitor's facial language, body language. You'll get a review of your performance by keeping an eye on your audience (which is true of all audiences—large or small, taped or "live"). How does that review match up with *your* analysis of yourself?

■

Videotapes offer the presenter one more reward, and it may be the most valuable one of all.

In the past, before videotape, presentations had very short lives.

They were given and they were gone. Presentations were ephemeral, evaporating into the atmosphere. *Poof!* There goes another presentation.

Now, with videotapes, presentations are *tangible*—preserved for as long as you please. The presenter has something to study, analyze, set aside, and consider again.

The tape *doesn't* evaporate.

Tapes are good, solid *tools* that you can use to upgrade your presentation skills—and maybe even your self-image.

Here's looking at you, kid!

56

Good news:
You'll never get a
bad evaluation.

To make a presentation and not get an evaluation is like running the Melrose Mile without a timer's clock. It is like playing baseball without a batting average—shooting a round of golf without a scorecard.

You've got to get an evaluation of your presentation if for no other reason than to know that you were in the game. A presentation that doesn't warrant an evaluation probably didn't make *any* impression.

Whoa! Before we get too dogmatic, let's define the field of play.

There are all kinds of evaluations—from a polite round of applause to a computerized form with grades, ratings, and multiple-choice answers.

Iron-clad rule: Whatever its configuration, wherever it comes from, welcome your evaluation with open arms! Clasp all kind words to your bosom and be thankful (same thing goes for unkind words, only it's tougher to do).

There are two reasons, basically, for going out of your way to obtain some valid kind of evaluation from your audience:

1. It's just human nature to want to know, *need to know*, how your audience felt about you.

2. An honest, constructive evaluation can be enormously helpful to you as you get ready for your next presentation. You'll have some idea of what worked and what didn't (that's why the more specific evaluations are always the most valuable).

In talking to program directors throughout the land, I have discovered that audiences register their evaluations in patterns of behavior that are sensible and frequently surprising:

A. There are the people who will come forward after a presentation and thank you for your effort. That's not easy for some people to do, so you want to let them know that their kind words mean a lot to you. Tennessee Williams said, "Why do people begrudge you a bit of praise?" When praise comes your way, *soak it up!*

Seldom, if ever, will people approach the presenter after a presentation and say critical things. Occasionally, a suggestion will be made, but generally in a positive way. I've never heard anyone say, "That was a *rotten* presentation. I was bored silly. Why don't you find a new subject to talk about?" It's quite possible that evaluations of that severity are warranted, but they aren't made—at least not face-to-face—right after a presentation.

B. The people who have harsh things to say about a presentation usually register then in a *non* face-to-face manner. If something that you said really *galled* some members of your audience, look for a written response—usually at the back of the room.

Chuck Kelly, an advertising executive in Minneapolis who is always a program chairman of at least one noteworthy organization, says, "People will write what bothers them and leave it at the back of the room. The comments are more likely to be emotional, sensitive to something that was *touched upon* in your presentation rather than to the main subject. Written comments, left behind, will probably be subjective rather than objective." Heated comments, it would seem, are more likely to be dashed off on the spot. But you know the rule: *welcome all forms of evaluation with open arms!*

C. Then, there's another group you should know about. These are the members of your audience who will take the time and trouble to fill out a form that has been dispatched to them after your presentation, or was picked up at the presentation and carried home. These forms can be demanding (there's a fairly simple one on the opposite page). Some organizations send out questionnaires, some don't, but here's the point:

Since time has elapsed between the presentation and the filling-out of the questionnaire, answers are likely to be dispassionate and thoughtful. This kind of evaluation, requiring recall, is going to put your presentation into a larger context than an evaluation made on the spot—and is likely to be more useful. These are considered judgments.

D. You've detected the gap, of course. What about those people who don't come forward, don't leave notes at the back of the room, don't take the trouble to fill out questionnaires.

They just get up and leave.

I've given these people a name: "The Movie Crowd." Here's a snapshot:

Have you ever watched people coming out of a theater after seeing a movie that you are waiting to see? You search their faces, seeking a clue—some slight reaction to the film they just saw. They reveal nothing. They just amble along.

They're not chattering happily. They're not muttering *un*happily. They're not storming the box office. They're just leaving.

One day, it came to me. A presumption on my part, but it seemed unarguable: *"Well, I guess they got their money's worth."*

PRESENTATION EVALUATION

Name of presenter _____

✔ Please rate the presentation on a scale of 10 (highest) to 1.	😁				🙂			😟		
	10	9	8	7	6	5	4	3	2	1
Relevant to my needs:										
Strength of material:										
Persuasiveness:										
Learn anything new?										
Delivery:										
Audio/Visual:										

Comments, reactions: _____

_____

_____

_____

_____

Signed: _____
(optional)

That blinding flash of obviousness has helped me at presentations ever since.

"The Movie Crowd" shows up, in varying numbers, at all manner of presentations. They come in, listen, *and leave*. They get their money's worth.

On the evaluation scale (10 being "ecstatic"), you can figure that they gave you a 6. You take it, *gratefully* (remember the rule).

There is one more way that an audience can register its evaluation of you, but it is so decisively different from all the rest that it deserves its own category. It happens only in competitive presentations.

The audience makes a commitment. They award you the contract, give you the account, approve the budget, declare you the winner.

These are specific actions. You know where you stand (particularly when you win; maybe not so clearly when you lose).

Try for specific evaluations. (See the suggested form at the end of this chapter. It doesn't require a lot of time, but it does ask for some thought and a fair degree of precision.)

Be particularly thankful when you get an evaluation that reflects some thoughtful effort, but keep in mind that *all* evaluations can be helpful. Even "The Movie Crowd" is telling you something. And the more feedback you get, the better you're going to be.

57

Presentations are changing dramatically, but *two* things never will.

Presentation is an ever-changing, never-changing form of communication.

The changes are all around us, engagingly evident wherever presentations are made.

■ Yes, there is more electronic gear to enlarge the presenter, resonate the voice, orchestrate the message, visualize the product, and do almost everything *wirelessly*.

■ Yes, there are more one-on-one presentations. One person sitting across a table or desktop from another. Often, the material they are discussing was created in a computer.

■ Yes, there are more meetings of all kinds. It seems like business executives "live" in meetings, watching presentations of all shades of quality. More and more, we seem to learn from *watching*.

■ Yes, meetings are shorter than they used to be (*some* of them, anyway), since time-consciousness equates with cost-consciousness. The long-winded presenter is shut down more routinely now.

■ Yes, television has had enormous impact on presentations and presenters. Almost instinctively, we visualize "live" presenters with video frames around their heads. We make subconscious comparisons between presenters we see in the office and Dan Rather on the tube.

■ Yes, we say that we are more alert to the thin line between style and substance, but most audiences have a devil of a time separating the two. The left brain (analytical) has been keeping company with the right brain (emotional) since the beginning of civilization.

So, presentations change—reflecting the changes in culture and communications technology—but *two* things don't change. Never have. And, most likely, never will.

1. *You must step forward and present yourself.* You must have the audacity, guts, ego, nerve, self-esteem—whatever it is, whatever it takes—to move center-stage, look your audience directly in the eye, and open up. "Well, here I am . . . this is how I turned out."

2. *You must give us something*—an idea, a direction, a proposal, a bit of inspiration, *something* your audience can use.

Point No. 1 in this extremely brief list of unchanging requirements of presentation is strictly up to you.

Point No. 2 is where this book has marched bravely into the breach—suggesting ideas that you can use to improve your next presentation. In the fervent belief that you can't have too many good ideas, the final chapter offers a few dozen more—in the now familiar form of *nuggets*. Dip into them. Circle some with a marker if you want. Paste one or two on your forehead. Do whatever *works* to help you make your next presentation the best presentation of your life.

58

"The next step is . . ."

Ten days before your next presentation, take this list full of nuggets on the next two pages and pin the whole glittering array to the wall of your office, den, kitchen, basement, or wherever you're going to be.

Add your own notes and nuggets as presentation day approaches. The night before your presentation, review each point (*visualize* it, if possible).

You'll discover that you feel remarkably comfortable about yourself as a presenter—and confident about your presentation.

So, flip this page and start thinking about your next presentation. You're going to be dazzling!

NUGGETS FOR YOUR NEXT PRESENTATION.

1 — Make a "hot button" seating sketch. Works well in small meetings. Set up your meeting so that seating is prearranged. Then, make your sketch—identifying each seat by the main concern of the person who will be sitting there. *Visualize each concern.*

2 — Most presentations are *two* things: (1) a solid base for; (2) an idea that relates directly to an audience need. Make sure you've got both.

3 — Fill your head with knowledge before you prepare your presentation. You should have at least *seven times* as much useful information as you will actually use.

4 — Close your presentation *strongly.* Ask your audience to do something specific. Leave something behind (a proposal, article, summary, checklist), something to remember you by.

5 — Rehearse everything exactly as it will be. Say every word. Make every move. Afterward, get a compassionate critique from your "Stanley Kubrick."

6 — Every question you get is an indication of interest. *Welcome it!*

7 — Be sensitive to the sensitivities of your audience. Identify their "nerve endings"—like age, gender, locality, "colloquialisms."

8 — Present yourself to yourself. A full-length mirror would be perfect.

9 — Shift, as quickly as you can, from self-consciousness to audience-consciousness. Put yourself in their shoes. It's the best way to beat nervousness.

10 — Use "you" whenever you can.

11 — State your point of view early on. Most people are too busy (or too smart) to be held in suspense for very long.

12 — Let your convictions show.

13
_____

- Substance is essential. Technique usually breaks down at the point where substance is thinnest, or ceases to exist. Great presentations are never made on technique alone. It's just not possible.

14
_____

- If you've got a sense of humor, it will blossom when you feel you really *know* your subject.

15
_____

- Use your humor, but don't wait for laughs.

16
_____

- Most people would rather say: "That presenter told me what I have long suspected to be true," than, "That person told me a lot of things I never heard before."

17
_____

- Offer lists (like this one).

18
_____

- If you can do your presentation *without* audio/visual aids, you'll cut nervousness way down. Reason: You won't be nearly as worried about an equipment breakdown.

19
_____

- If you're using cards or charts, you don't have to cover one with another. One advantage of cards is that they can be placed around a room to help your audience remember where you've taken them.

20
_____

- Never give a "generic presentation." Localize it. Personalize it. Relate it to the news of the day.

21
_____

- Watch for "the barometer" in the audience. There's usually *one person* who reacts more quickly and demonstrably than the others. Let that person help you anticipate the overall reactions.

22
_____

- Get out of the gray—demonstrate. Use audio/visual aids that give you freedom. Improvise within your knowledge. Don't break eye contact for more than ten seconds.

23
_____

- Be more of your strongest strength. Put your faith in what you like best about yourself—and your weaknesses will fade away.

24
_____

- Keep looking for ways to crystallize issues, so that varying views can reach areas of agreement. "Isn't *this* what everybody's saying?"

Suggested Reading

- Attenborough, Richard. *A Chorus Line*. New York: New American Library, 1985
- Boettinger, Henry M. *Moving Mountains—or The Art of Letting Others See Things Your Way*. New York: Collier Books, 1969.
- Calamandrei, Piero. *Eulogy of Judges*. New Jersey: Princeton University Press, 1946.
- Detz, Joan. *How to Write and Give a Speech*. New York: St. Martin's Press, 1984.
- Goffman, Erving. *The Presentation of Self in Everyday Life*. New York: Doubleday & Company, Inc., 1959.
- Hodgson, John and Ernest Richards. *Improvisation*. New York: Grove Press, Inc., 1966, 1974.
- Leech, Thomas. *How to Prepare, Stage, and Deliver Winning Presentations*. New York: Amacom—American Management Associations, 1982.
- Morris, Desmond. *Bodywatching*. New York: Crown Publishers, Inc., 1985.
- Nizer, Louis. *Reflections Without Mirrors*. New York: Doubleday & Company, Inc., 1978.
- Rusher, William A. *How to Win Arguments*. New York: Doubleday & Company, Inc., 1981.
- Samuels, Mike, M.D., and Nancy Samuels. *Seeing With the Mind's Eye*. New York: Random House, Inc., 1975.
- Schanker, Harry H. *The Spoken Word*. New York: McGraw-Hill, Inc., 1982.
- Thourlby, William. *You Are What You Wear*. Kansas City: Sheed Andrews and McMeel, 1978.
- von Oech, Roger. *A Kick in the Seat of the Pants*. New York: Harper & Row, 1986.
- Valenti, Jack. *Speak Up With Confidence*. New York: William Morrow & Company, Inc., 1982.

Index